ILLUSTRATING CHILDREN'S BOOKS

ILLUSTRATING CHILDREN'S BOOKS

A GUIDE TO DRAWING, PRINTING, AND PUBLISHING

Nancy S. Hands

PRENTICE HALL PRESS
New York   London   Toronto   Sydney   Tokyo

With thanks for
  the encouragement and help
    of Jay, Eric, and Kara

Published by Prentice Hall Press
A Division of Simon & Schuster, Inc.
Gulf + Western Building
One Gulf + Western Plaza
New York, NY 10023

PRENTICE HALL PRESS is a trademark of Simon & Schuster, Inc.

Library of Congress Cataloging in Publication Data

Hands, Nancy S.
  Illustrating children's books.

  (The Art & design series)
  Includes bibliographies and index.
  1. Illustration of books—Technique.   2. Illustrated
books, Children's—Marketing.   I. Title.   II. Series.
NC965.H36   1986   741.64'2   85-28133
ISBN 0-13-451402-5

Manufactured in the United States of America

10   9   8   7   6   5   4   3

Acknowledgments

Thanks for the special help of: Tony Chin, University of Minnesota Photo Lab; Leanne Dillingham, Raintree Publications; Andy Gilats, Split Rock Arts Program; Karen Hoyle, University of Minnesota Libraries; Jay Johnson, Carnival Enterprises; Leslie Lang, Riverside Color Corporation; Susan Pearson, Carolrhoda Books; Jerry Rockman, Worzalla Publishing.

Thanks to the artists who gave their time to write or talk to me about their work: Mary Azarian, Marcia Brown, Eric Carle, Donald Carrick, Barbara Cooney, Julie Downing, Ed Emberly, Fritz Eichenberg, Leonard Everett Fisher, Stephen Gammell, Diane Goode, Gail Haley, Arnold Lobel, Charles Mikolaycak, Ed Young, Margot Zemach, and especially Uri Shulevitz.

Contents

Introduction

FIGURE 0.1. Randolph Caldecott: *The Diverting Ride of John Gilpin* (William Cowper). Wood engraving. *(Reprinted by permission of Frederick Warne and Co., Inc.)*

"...the illustrator is an artist whose education knows no beginning and no end.... Every book should be a thing of beauty aimed at permanency."

FRITZ EICHENBERG,
The Illustrator's Notebook

The illustrator of children's books is faced with the unique challenge of combining fine and graphic arts skills with the ability to communicate to children. Each person working in the field must consider several important questions: "Do I spend hours reading and delighting in children's books?" "Am I in touch with a child's way of viewing the world?" "Do I believe that I have something positive to contribute to children through my art?" If you answer these questions affirmatively, then you can use this book as a take-off point for developing your skills.

Each chapter provides an overview of the areas of knowledge the illustrator must know well in order to succeed in this exciting field. Integrated throughout the text are exercises designed to give practical experience in solving illustration problems unique to children's books. Completion of the exercises

FIGURE 0.2. Fritz Eichenberg: *Rainbows are Made: Poems by Carl Sandburg*, selected by Lee Bennet Hopkins. Wood engraving for "Elm Buds."

will result in a body of work that can be used in a portfolio to show publishers. Further resources for extended study are provided at the back of the book. You will become familiar with the history of the field, contemporary illustrators and markets, types of children's books, the printing process, preparing art for print, and presenting work to publishers. And, most important, using this book will help you assess the areas in which you may need study or practice.

Every person brings a unique set of experiences and special strengths to illustrating for children. In making the best use of this book for your own needs and background, read the entire book once to gain a whole perspective. Then, return to the chapters and exercises on which you feel you need to spend more time working on specific skills. The exercises have been designed to provide practice in working out problems you may encounter when actually illustrating a children's book. If your interest in children's book illustration comes from your parenting or teaching experiences and you have no formal art training, you will learn exactly what skills you will need to develop. Treat this book as a map that shows a variety of roads to reach an end point. Evaluate how much time you need to spend on any one road be-

fore you reach your final destination.

Study the art chosen for the book to see the variety of techniques, subjects, and approaches to illustrating for children. Examples of art in its preparatory stages have been included so that you can see some of the processes the artist went through before arriving at the best solution for a given page. Compare these studies with the final printed versions by checking these books out of your local library. Although each illustration chosen for the book is distinct, some common threads bind them together. The pieces of art reveal a vitality and honesty that reflect the artist's underlying respect for an audience that deserves the best.

Once you have gained an understanding of children's books, it becomes clear that the best art and writing are not merely a matter of attaining technical skills. The finest illustrators and authors have reached inside themselves to retrieve their own childhood experiences and feelings to communicate with children today. Their art is inspired by their individual visions of the world, combined with their closeness to their own childhood. As you use the material in this book, take time to reflect upon your own childhood and draw upon its richness to bring your best to today's children.

Finding Out
Where You Fit in

FIGURE 1.1. Barbara Cooney: *Ox-Cart Man* (Donald Hall). Acrylics. "He packed potatoes they dug from their garden. . . ."

"I like books that remain faithful to the essence of art; namely, those that offer children an intuitive and direct way of knowledge, a simple beauty capable of being perceived immediately, arousing in their soul a vibration which will endure all their lives."

PAUL HAZARD,
Books, Children, and Men

USING THIS CHAPTER

The purpose of this chapter is to acquaint you with children's books and to stimulate your thinking about what books can offer to children. If you have a limited knowledge of the variety of books that are being produced for children today, the activities in this chapter will give you a perspective on contemporary books for children. Knowing the field well is the first step toward finding out where you might apply your own skills and creativity.

WHAT CHILDREN'S BOOKS CAN MEAN TO A CHILD

Children may experience an unknown world through books. In *Ox-Cart Man,* written by Donald Hall and illustrated by Barbara Cooney, children learn how a family in nineteenth-century America worked together to supply their daily needs. The illustrations have enough detail to offer children a historical perspective. They complement a poetic text that is rich with material to stimulate discussion about life then and now. (See Figure 1.1.)

Sometimes the unknown world in a children's book is an imaginary place. Fantasy can serve the purpose of allowing children to express emotions they may usually hide, as in the urge to run away that is expressed by Max's adventure in *Where the Wild Things Are.* (See Plate 8.) The successful fantasies parallel reality closely enough so that the child can understand what is happening. Fantasy also may spark a creative urge in the child. The reading of William Pène Du Bois's *Twenty-One Balloons,* for example, may stimulate a string of unique inventions.

Through the characters in children's books, children identify their own emotions. Children read about Frog and Toad, the marvelous characters created by Arnold Lobel, and see their own daily problems. Perhaps the child has also lost a button from a jacket or has been recently reprimanded for eating too many cookies. (See Figure 1.2.)

Books can also help children understand their own environments. A city child who feels confined by apartment living may be inspired by the imagination of the boy in *One Monday Morning,* by Uri Shulevitz. After reading this book, children may be able to look at their surroundings in a new way. (See Figure 1.3.)

The art in children's books helps the child develop a sense of aesthetics. Book illustrations may be the young child's primary source of exposure to art. Consequently, artists must accept the responsibility to give children their highest conception of what is beautiful. Today's children are bombarded with a multitude of visual stimuli characteristic of an electronic age. In order to make aesthetic choices later in life, children need to be exposed to quality in art at an early age.

Illustrations also serve as an impetus to lead the child into reading. Children look at the pictures and talk about what is happening in a book. Soon they may recognize some of the words they have spoken. In books illustrated for older children, compelling artwork invites the reader to ponder particular events in a story. Imaginative illustrations may add another level of meaning to the text, giving more for the reader to think about.

This positive impact of art in children's books can be felt only if the art reflects the involvement of the artist in the book's creation. The illustrations cannot be lifeless images, carelessly executed. Neither should they

(Reprinted by permission of Harper & Row, Inc.)

FIGURE 1.2. Arnold Lobel: *Frog and Toad Together.* Ink wash in three-color hand separations. "These are the best cookies I have ever eaten!" said Frog.

(Reprinted by permission of
Charles Scribner's Sons)

FIGURE 1.3. Uri Shulevitz: *One Monday Morning*. Ink washes in four colors, hand separated, tailpiece.

be inaccurate portrayals of the text. An illustrator must take the time necessary to absorb a text and arrive at an original vision. We can never expect to know which detail of a drawing or portrayal of a character will affect a child at a given moment. Yet, every book offers the chance to create images that can enrich children's lives and remain in their minds throughout adulthood. Can you still recapture the intimate feelings engendered by Beatrix Potter's portrayal of Peter Rabbit? (See Figure 1.4) Do you ever smile when you see a huge pile of doughnuts because your mind has flashed back to *Homer Price* and Uncle Ulysses's nonstop doughnut-making machine? (See Figure 1.5.)

FIGURE 1.4. Beatrix Potter. Drawing from a letter to Noel Moore.

FIGURE 1.5. Robert McCloskey: *Homer Price*. Lithographic crayon. "... and the doughnuts kept right on rolling down the little chute, all ready to eat."

QUALITIES OF GOOD CHILDREN'S BOOK ILLUSTRATION

Good art does not necessarily make good illustration. An artist can paint a beautiful picture of fall trees, but unless this painting makes an idea clearer, it will not fulfill the function of an illustration. The art also must be executed in a way that will reproduce well. Good illustration goes beyond exact rendering of the words, to offer an interpretation of them. The illustrator uses all the graphic elements of line, color, texture, compositon, and even page size, to relate to the intention of the book.

Although excellent art may not make excellent illustration, excellent illustration must be excellent art. The examples cited throughout this book and the illustrations chosen for inclusion fulfill this requirement. Children's book illustrators must be able to draw well and use their chosen medium expertly. Technical mastery, however, should never replace content or diminish the warmth of a book.

The best illustrators have a subtle sensitivity to language. Maurice Sendak speaks about his own affinity with words, which feels totally natural. He likens this experience to a composer thinking of music when he reads a poem.[1] Sendak and other interpretive illustrators speak of their role as finding a space within the text to let the pictures take over. As a result, the artist reaches for a new dimension to bring to the words. The illustrations move beyond mere decorations or

11

literal portrayals of an action. In Plate 8, Sendak includes a piece of cake on the table. The text does not state anything about the mother's feelings, but the piece of cake indicates the mother's enduring love for Max.

A special requirement of children's book illustration is that it communicate to children. Adults often disagree on what is appropriate art for children. Although children respond to a great many styles and mediums, some common qualities characterize the best art for children. For very young children the art should be simple and direct so that they can immediately understand the images. Older children have the ability to absorb many details and look for action and vivid portrayals of characters. Whatever age the book is designed for, its art must offer children a fresh and positive outlook on the world. For many artists this means reaching back into their own childhoods for inspiration. Perhaps your childhood sense of curiosity has never been far below the surface. You walk through the woods seeing faces in gnarled trees, or you have trouble restraining yourself from climbing over high fences in order to discover what is on the other side. Use your own sense of wonder and hope and you will surely be able to communicate to your intended audience.

EVALUATING CHILDREN'S BOOKS

The following activities are designed to help you evaluate children's books and to gain a general familiarity with them. As you study the books, make your own file card system to record your responses to individual books. Include the names of the author, artist, publisher, and the original publication date on the file cards. You will find the publishing information useful for an activity suggested

later in the book. Your responses to the books will form the beginning of your own approach to illustrating for children. Begin by becoming familiar with your local library's children's section. As you read and study a variety of books, answer the following questions to aid your evaluation process.

Point of View

What is the author's and illustrator's point of view? Is it positive? Does it seem to be from a child's perspective? Does the author/illustrator involve the child in the art and the story?

Mood

What is the overall tone of the book? How did the illustrator achieve this mood through the use of color, style of art, pacing the illustrations, or format of the pages? Does the mood of the art harmonize with the feeling of the words?

Technique

Why do you think the artist chose this particular technique? Was the technique used effectively? How does the technique help convey the mood of the text? Note the wide variety of mediums used in children's book illustration. Do you see any that don't seem suitable for children? Which techniques appeal to you the most? Why? Which reflect your own strengths as an artist?

Pacing

Is the book's pacing effective? What makes you want to turn the pages? What makes you want to linger over a page? Do the illustrations have enough variety to maintain interest? Is there a natural movement from one page to the next?

Illustrations as Problem Solving

How does the artist's style change with the demands of a particular text? To answer this question you will need to study the works of several illustrators who have illustrated many books. Look at each book to see if the artistic response to the text seems to be a unique solution to the particular story or whether a formula has been applied to the art for each book. Some excellent artists to study for creative solutions to each text are: Marcia Brown, Barbara Cooney, William Pène DuBois, Roger Duvosin, Nonny Hogrogian, Leon Lionni, Maurice Sendak, Uri Shulevitz, and Leonard Weisgard.

Once you have completed your library study, move to the best local book store that carries a large selection of children's books. The library collection will give you a perspective on books that have stood the test of time. The bookstore will feature what is being published and promoted today. Unfortunately, there are not enough general bookstores with large, well-chosen children's book sections, but the growth of excellent children's book specialty stores is a positive sign that quality children's books are becoming more widely available. Search for the best your area has to offer and continue your evaluation process. This will help you discover how your work might fit in to what is being published currently.

One additional place to get another perspective on children's book illustration is your local discount store, drugstore, or supermarket. These stores sell mass-produced and mass-marketed books. Apply the same standards to these books that you did to the books in the library and bookstore. Look to see if there is a variety in the art, in-depth characterizations, and satisfying content. Take note of the printing quality and materials used in the books' manufacturing.

Keep your notes in a file box so that you may add to them as you progress in your study of children's books. They will be helpful in further activities for studying techniques and for identifying publishers you wish to contact.

A final activity to add another dimension to your evaluations is to read reviews of children's books. Several periodicals regularly review children's literature, and these are listed in the Resources section for this chapter that begins on page 155. Although the focus is often on the writing, you may apply the same standards to the art.

A Special Kind
of Drawing

FIGURE 2.1. Robert Lawson: *The Treasure of the Isle Mist* (W. W. Tarn). Pen and ink, half-title for chapter four.

"The life an an illustrator, I am sure, is an endless process of observing and storing away in some curious ragbag part of his mind all the thousands of ill-assorted facts and impressions that he will someday be called upon to use...."

ROBERT LAWSON,
Robert Lawson: Illustrator

USING THIS CHAPTER

This chapter provides exercises that will help gear your drawing to the content in children's books. Although the subjects of children's books are diverse, certain commonalities call for particular drawing skills. The first requirement is to be able to draw well. Your drawing must also possess a vitality that captures the frequent scenes and activities portrayed in children's books.

If you have had art training, chances are your drawing did not focus on the subjects common to children's books. The activities in this chapter will give you new material to add to your portfolio. If you have not drawn regularly for a long time, the exercises will limber up a rusty hand and sharpen your eyes to see in the special way that drawing demands. If you have never had formal art training, the exercises will offer you a way to begin drawing and will suggest a direction for you to pursue through further self-study or course work.

The purpose of this chapter is not to teach you how to draw but to suggest what to draw through the exercises. If you are at the beginning stages of learning to draw, use this chapter in conjunction with one of the books in the Resources section that is designed to teach you how to draw. A self-evaluation exercise at the end of the chapter will help you assess your drawing after you have completed the exercises.

Children are quick to note any discrepancy between art and text. They feel cheated if something is not correct. The imagination and feelings that artists impart to their drawings, combined with a care that is reflected in every detail of a drawing, can be the mechanisms that draw a child into a book.

THE SKETCHBOOK

Your sketchbook is an important tool for daily drawing. Keep an ongoing sketchbook to help your drawing stay fluid and to record moments that can serve as a reference for finished drawings. Your sketchbook may also be a source for characters and scenes in future books. Faithfully drawing in your sketchbook will increase your powers of observation, which will lead to accurate recording of images. If you spend one hour a day drawing a three-year-old at play, you will come to understand how a three-year-old's body is put together and the child's typical movements and posture. This understanding will be transferred to your drawings.

Sketchbooks come in many sizes, with various grades of paper. Choose a sketchbook of a comfortable size, such as nine by twelve inches, to enable you to carry it with you at all times. One with inexpensive paper will encourage you to draw quickly and prolifically. Make sure that the quality of paper is compatible with the drawing tools you like to use. Newsprint, for example, is not suitable for felt-tip marker drawing because the marker bleeds onto the next sheets of paper. Select drawing materials that enable you to work quickly and freely. Pencils, graphite sticks, drawing pens, and felt-tip markers work well because they are portable and lend themselves to quick sketching.

Purchase several sketchbooks of different sizes to use for various purposes. A trip to the zoo to capture animals in movement requires large paper in order to record a variety of poses on a single sheet. (See Figure 2.2.)

Use your sketchbook as a tool to keep your drawing loose and to record moments

FIGURE 2.2. Nancy S. Hands. Pen and ink. Sparky the seal at the St. Paul Como Zoo.

FIGURE 2.3. Nancy S. Hands. Pencil sketch of "Turk's Cap" lily.

that might otherwise be lost. Finished drawings can be worked on later, but you may never be able to duplicate the moment of a little girl's swagger when she first tries on a pair of high heels and struts across the living room. You can also use the sketchbook as a reference source to record visual details that form the basis of future drawings. For example, a walk in the woods can be used to make detailed drawings of wildflowers, where parts are labeled and colors noted. These studies will be accurate enough to provide the material for a future assignment of

a drawing that requires wildflowers. (See Figure 2.3.)

SKETCHBOOK EXERCISES
Capturing Gesture and Movement

The purpose of the following exercises is to help you develop a lively style of drawing. The best drawings in children's books have vitality. Editors look for this quality when reviewing portfolios. The subjects of the exercises are children and animals.

Exercise 1: Children at Play

Go to a location where you can easily and unobtrusively observe young children playing. If you are a parent, you may be more successful in drawing children not related to you, because you will be free of interruptions and can concentrate on your subjects. However, there will be times when your own children may serve as perfect subjects for this type of exercise. Moments when they are absorbed in play in a sandbox or busy splashing water in a wading pool are great times to bring out the sketchbook. Be prepared for your subjects to be in constant motion, and be clear that your task is to capture movement. Do not expect children to be still to provide perfect poses for detailed drawings. If you have never drawn people in motion, your task will seem difficult at first. Concentrate in the few seconds that you do have to capture a pose. Your goal should be to catch the essence of that pose in a few lines, rather than to make a complete drawing.

Begin your drawing session by taking time to observe a child long enough to learn how the child moves. Watch closely how arms and legs move. Try to feel with your own body the particular stance of the child. As children play they usually repeat the same movements over and over; for example, climbing up the steps of a slide, sliding down, and then running to climb up again. Choose one entire movement to focus on and look for the part of the movement that you think will translate best into drawing. Close your eyes, visualize the movement in your mind (you may see an afterimage), and then quickly record what you have seen on paper.[1] By the time you are ready to draw, the child probably will have moved to another position. But if you can learn to retain the original movement in your mind, it will help

you to record it on paper. Now return to the child and keep watching. When the child returns to the recorded movement, you may have a chance to check the accuracy of your drawing. Then fill in more details through further observation and from what you know about how a child's body is constructed.

There are several methods that you can use to record an image quickly. Small gesture drawings are helpful for warming up in a drawing session. Use loose wrist movements to capture the essential posture. Figure 2.4 shows some quick, small gesture drawings of a child at play. Working small enables you to concentrate on the general pose rather than on details. It also allows you to record several poses on one sheet as the child changes position. You may, however, feel less restricted if you work on large drawings, because you can get your whole body into the action as you draw. Try both large and small gesture drawings to see which method works best for you.

Another method of working is to record the feeling of a pose by building up a tonal mass using crayon, graphite sticks, charcoal, or brush and wash. Experiment with some of these mediums to record the essence of a movement quickly and without detail. (See Figure 2.5.)

Once you have completed these warm-up exercises, you may return to the drawings and begin to fill in details. This can be done by further observation or at home. If you like to use pencil, the first drawings can be done lightly or with a hard lead. Details can then be drawn on top later using a darker, or a softer, lead. You can also use lines over wash and crayon tonal mass drawings. (See Figure 2.6.) Another way to fill in more detail is to keep working on the same poses on a single sheet as the subject returns to a previous position. After studying the child's typical move-

FIGURE 2.4. Nancy S. Hands. Gesture sketches of child playing.

FIGURE 2.5. Nancy S. Hands. Tonal mass gesture sketches of child.

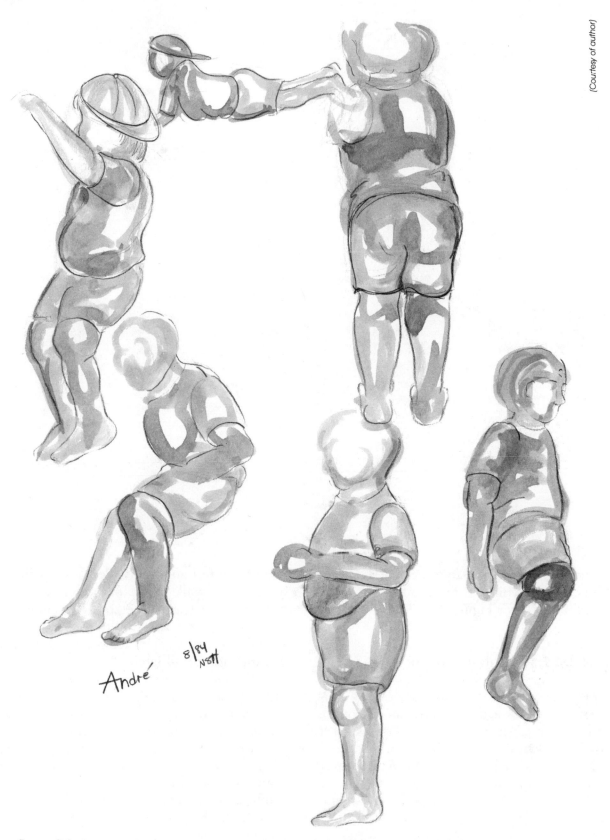

André   8/84
                NSH

FIGURE 2.6. Nancy S. Hands. Wash drawings with pencil details added of a child playing.

FIGURE 2.7. Nancy S. Hands. Pencil sketches of a child in movement.

ments, you can pick four or five poses to work on, switching from pose to pose as the child moves. (See Figure 2.7.)

Exercise 2: Animals in Motion

Apply the same instructions for drawing children at play to recording animals in motion. If you own a pet, your pet is a good subject to begin with because you have unconsciously observed the pet's movement over time. Your knowledge of your pet will be translated into your drawings. If you do not have a pet, begin by drawing an animal for whom you feel an affinity. Perhaps it will require just a walk to the park, a ride to the country, or a trip to the zoo. Remember to study the motions first and to capture the essential gestures quickly. Keep your drawings free and add detail later.

If there is a zoo in or near your community, try several lengthy visits for drawing. You may discover an animal you never thought about drawing before to make this exercise filled with fun. (Figure 2.8 is from Prairie Dog town at the Duluth Zoo.) Your drawing sessions will pay off in artwork that is infused with life and may provide the basis for a future book.

Figure 2.8. Nancy S. Hands. Pencil sketches of prairie dogs at the Duluth Zoo.

Recording Environments

Settings in children's books are crucial to the success of the illustrations. An illustrator must create a sense of place. The feeling of a particular room or landscape may be just what draws the child into the book. The best drawings create a sense of intimacy when depicting a story's setting. (In Plate 8 from *Where the Wild Things Are,* Maurice Sendak has created an intimate interior scene; while in Plate 9 from *The Treasure,* Uri Shulevitz invites the child into an outdoor environment.)

Once you start thinking about the possible scenarios that can go into future books, the world will never seem quite the same to you. If you walk into a library and notice an antique chair with elaborately carved legs, your mind may start to imagine a prince sitting on the comfortably warm leather. During a walk in the woods, you may see a distinctively gnarled tree that has become the habitat of many little animals. Perhaps some day that tree will become part of a book. Take time to record the objects and settings that intrigue you as you go through your daily activities. If you do not have the time to make a detailed drawing at the moment you encounter something interesting, make a written note of it and return to draw it when you do have time.

Exercise 3: Drawing Outdoor Environments

A good starting point for drawing outdoors is to take extra time to observe what is around you and then record the details. All drawings begin with seeing. Drawing for children may require you to see your world from a new perspective. How would a large

tree look if you were less than half your present height? Try to imagine what aspects of a setting would capture a child's imagination. Is there a house in your neighborhood that has the air of being haunted? Does a hill where you walk your dog just beg to be rolled down? What settings appeal to the fanciful side of your own nature? Find these places and then start drawing.

Once you have chosen an outdoor area to draw, you will have to make decisions about what to include or exclude from your drawings if you plan to develop them into a finished drawing that would be suitable for an illustration. You can use your outdoor drawing experiences not only to practice drawing and recording interesting settings, but also to develop skills in composing a picture page. After studying an appealing scene, try to imagine this scene as being an important setting in a book. Look at Stephen Gammell's pencil landscape drawing in Figure 2.9. The illustration suggests the mood of the writing. Try drawing a setting in such a way that you are emphasizing a chosen mood. Will there be rain clouds looming above the trees and darks emphasized? Is it a peaceful moment flooded with sunlight? What part of the setting do you wish to emphasize? How will you do this? Through an unusual perspective? By enlarging a building?

Another benefit of recording outdoor environments is that you can take all the time you need to draw details such as tree bark textures or brick patterns in buildings. When you are ready to work on a final drawing, you can selectively use these details to achieve a particular effect.

One other possibility that is a positive benefit of drawing outdoor environments is that your imagination may become kindled in a special place. Your drawings could be

FIGURE 2.9. Stephen Gammell. Pencil landscape study.

the basis for the setting of a fantasy. You can start with what you see and add imaginary details to create a setting that will grab a child's imagination just as it grabbed yours.

Take time to look carefully at the world around you and use what you see to practice drawing with correct perspective, using successful picture composition, drawing for accuracy, and stretching your imagination.

Exercise 4: Drawing Indoor Environments

Interior environments are often crucial in establishing the atmosphere of a children's book. Good drawings contain enough detail to create a feeling of reality—whether the story is located in a real or imagined place. Children need to feel that they are *somewhere*. In picture books the economy of the

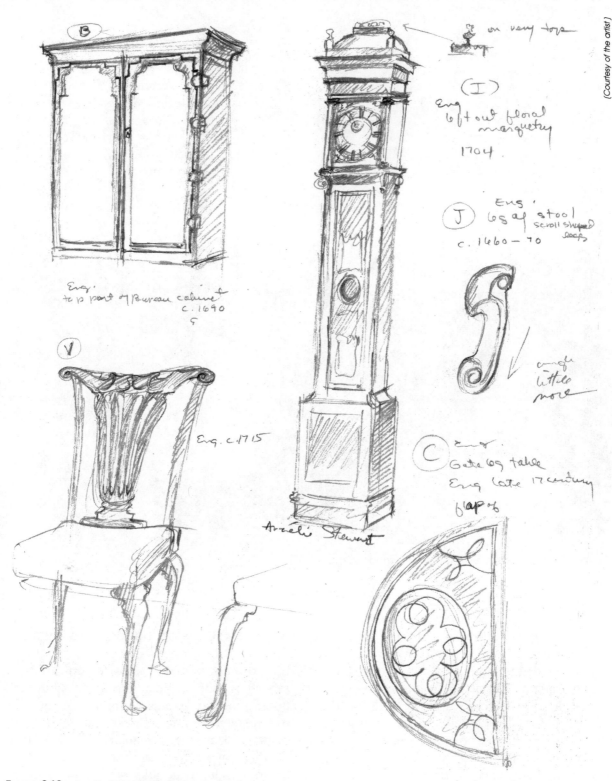

FIGURE 2.10. Arzelie Stewart. Sketchbook drawing.

language allows an illustrator to fill in many visual details that are omitted from the text.

For your sketchbook exercises, consider every interior environment you enter as your laboratory—whether it is a crowded bus, your kitchen, or a period room in a museum. Try drawing parts of your house that you may never have considered drawing before: the cellar stairway, the inside of a closet, your bathroom sink. Draw the same room from several different vantage points: Imagine yourself to be very small looking up at the big objects, draw from the doorway looking into a room, draw from the bottom step of a stairway facing up.

When you visit friends who live in a house or an apartment built in a different time period from your own home, draw the fixtures there. Draw the inside of your doctor's office while you are waiting for an appointment, the inside of your neighbor's

barn, or the shelves inside the corner store. If you carry your sketchbook with you at all times, you will find your days filled with countless opportunities to record indoor scenes. Each sketch will provide reference material, sharpen your powers of observation, and add to your ability to record what is around you. (See Figures 2.10 and 2.11 from Arzelie Stewart's sketchbook, which serves as a source for many varied indoor settings.)

Creating a Character

Most children's books require that the artist portray a character. The characters of children's books may be people or animals, real or imaginary. They express every type of emotion and engage in all types of activities. The artist must develop a character similar to

FIGURE 2.11. Arzelie Stewart. Sketchbook drawing.

(Courtesy of the artist)

the way the writer must develop a character. A character must be consistent and convincing. If you are accustomed to doing single drawings of people or animals, it may require an entirely different skill to draw people or animals in a variety of poses and with different facial expressions. The following drawing activities will give you practice in developing this skill.

Exercise 5: Creating a Child Character

Draw a child. Next draw the same child in a sequence of actions, experiencing different emotions. When you draw the child happy, sad, surprised, mad, or excited, convey the emotion through the child's entire body posture as well as through facial expressions.

Return to your sketches for Exercise 1 for help in this exercise. You may have to do more drawings of children at play to complete this exercise. This time, focus on expressions and gestures in your quick drawings. It may take many hours of drawing before you feel that you are able to create a child character successfully.

Look at several types of books to see how artists have depicted different characters in a variety of situations. George Karn's cartoon illustration (see Figure 2.12) records two of the many emotions that Melissa Sue McCormack experiences in Carol Marron's humorous story *Mother Told Me So*. Figure 2.13 shows Donald Carrick's realistic pen-and-ink sketches as he worked on developing the medieval boy character in *Harald and the Giant Knight*. Your own study of children's

FIGURE 2.12. George Karn: *Mother Told Me So* (Carol Marron). Pen and ink and tempera.

or let her balloons float away.

She didn't get caught in
the monkeyhouse turnstile,
or locked in a bathroom stall.

FIGURE 2.13. Donald Carrick: *Harald and the Giant Knight.* Pen and ink sketches.

books will reveal many other excellent examples of characterization.

Once you have developed your own child character and have engaged the character in a variety of actions, you can develop a setting for the character. If it is wintertime, invent outdoor clothes and a snowy scene. Draw the child's home and neighborhood. Keep elaborating, creating friends and family for your child character. Try this exercise using more than one style. Perhaps you will surprise yourself by creating a humorous cartoon character when usually your drawings

tend to be realistic and serious. All of these drawings will provide excellent material to develop later when you feel ready to prepare a portfolio.

Try the same exercise with an adult character who would appeal to children. Stephen Gammell's Old MacDonald (see Figure 3.5) is such a character. Priscilla Kiedrowski's sketches for her portrayal of Benjamin Franklin (see Figures 2.14 and 2.15) show some of the development Ben went through as she worked on his characterization for *Ben Franklin's Glass Armonica.*

FIGURE 2.14. Priscilla Kiedrowski. *Ben Franklin's Glass Armonica* (Bryna Stevens). Pencil sketches.

(Courtesy of the artist)

Exercise 6: Creating an Animal Character

Creating an animal character, just as with the child character, begins with careful observation. The better you understand the special qualities of your subject, the more convincing your drawings will be. Begin this exercise by making realistic studies of the animal you choose. Do a variety of quick drawings, recording many poses. Next, spend some time filling in details so that you have plenty of visual information to use in later drawings. Draw the animal in its natural habitat. (Read about some of its habits if you are unfamiliar with the life cycle of the animal.) Think about whether you wish to make your animal realistic or cartoonlike. If you choose a cartoon portrayal, whatever simplification or humorous characteristics you give the animal must be based on the animal's actual charcteristics. Using the animal's natural qualities is what will make a fictional animal convincing. Linda Escher's cartoon illustraton for Figure 2.16 uses a cat's penchant for rats to create a humorous drawing. In Figure 2.17, she records a squirrel in its natural habitat.

FIGURE 2.15. Priscilla Kiedrowski. *Ben Franklin's Glass Armonica* (Bryna Stevens). Pencil sketches.

(Courtesy of the artist)

(Reprinted by permission of the artist)

FIGURE 2.16. Linda Escher. Pen and ink drawing of cat.

If you have created a fictional character, add appropriate clothing and create a home for the animal. Invent some comrades. If you have chosen to do a realistic portrayal, make a series of drawings of your animal in its natural habitat engaged in its typical activities.

Interpretive Drawing

The previous exercises dealt with straightforward skills that continued practice will help develop. The ability to interpret words in a text is an allusive skill that is also required of the illustrator. An illustrator must understand words, their subtle meanings and implications, and be able to communicate this understanding in the drawings. This sensitivity to language is developed through a love of reading and the ability to search within one's self to arrive at a unique vision for a

FIGURE 2.17. Linda Escher. Pen and ink drawing of a squirrel.

(Reprinted by permission of the artist)

In *The Story of Ferdinand,* by Munro Leaf, Robert Lawson plays upon expectations that a bull will be ferocious in his characterization of Ferdinand. Ernest Shepard's characterizations of the stuffed animals in *Winnie the Pooh* work so well because they are consistent with the qualities of the real animals. Some other notable animal characterizations to look at are Louis Darling's Ralph S. Mouse in Beverly Cleary's *The Mouse and the Motor Cycle* and *Runaway Ralph,* Garth Williams's Chester the pig, and Charlotte the spider in E. B. White's *Charlotte's Web.*

text. The first step in the specific process of illustrating a piece of writing is to read and understand the work well. Next must come much thought. The role of interpreter of words presents to artists a challenge that can be one of the most satisfying aspects of creating art for children. It demands total involvement and stretching the imagination.

Exercise 7: Interpreting a Passage

For this exercise, select a favorite book that you have strong positive memories about from childhood or use something that you have written yourself. First read the whole book to absorb its general feeling. Think about the characters as you read. Make notes about what actions you may want to portray. Listen to the quiet parts of the story and look for the most dramatic moments.

Now select one passage to illustrate. What is the primary feeling in this piece of writing? Is it tense? Is there potential for humor? Can you feel something happening at the moment that isn't precisely described in the story? What part of the action do you wish to emphasize? These are some of the questions to consider while thinking about how you are going to approach the illustration. Look for where the words have left room for you to enter your own reactions to what is happening through your drawing.

In Figure 2.18, Jim LaMarche creates a mood that captures the feeling in a moment in Emily Crofford's text from *A Matter of Pride*. Try to use every element of your drawing to communicate the feeling of the words. Do several interpretations of the same passage and analyze each to see which works the best. Perhaps you will combine elements of several drawings to come up with the best

FIGURE 2.18. Jim LaMarche: *A Matter of Pride* (Emily Crofford). Pen and ink and wash. "You mean you're going to quit?"

interpretation. Begin by using pencil, so that you will feel free to make changes. When you feel satisfied with your drawing, develop it into a final conception using a black-and-white medium that you feel comfortable with and that best suits the passage. Repeat the process with another passage from the same or a different story. Each piece of writing will present a new challenge.

It is valuable to take one popular story and see how several illustrators have interpreted it. Little Red Riding Hood, for example, has been illustrated since the nineteenth century and continues to have modern versions, such as the recent edition by Trina Schart Hyman.

The illustration of poetry offers the chance to do interpretive drawings. Once you have illustrated a passage from a story, look at illustrations for poetry and then try some of your own versions of well-liked

(Reprinted by permission of Carolrhoda Books, Inc.)

FIGURE 2.19. Peter Hanson: *The Cat Walked Through the Casserole and Other Poems* (Pamela Espelund and Marilyn Waniek). Pen and ink: "Luck."

poems. In Figure 2.19, Peter Hanson's illustration for "Luck" in *The Cat Walked Through the Casserole* (Pamela Espeland and Marilyn Waniek) shows warm and reassuring feelings of a family with an adopted child.

RESEARCH FOR DRAWING

Whether you illustrate a nonfiction book that requires precise drawings to explain how a computer works or a fantasy picture book about a goose, accurate drawing is essential. Not even a small detail should be incorrect.

Artists must take the time necessary to collect accurate visual information for their drawings. This may be time consuming, but it is also fun and rewarding.

The experiences of Robert McCloskey in preparing his drawings for Caldecott Award-winning *Make Way for Ducklings* demonstrate both the hard work and fun. To learn about ducks, McCloskey visited the American Museum of Natural History to draw stuffed ducks. He did anatomical duck drawings at a library. He sought out an ornithologist in order to find books to read about the habits of ducks and to learn more about duck wings, bills, and feet. Perhaps his biggest adventure was purchasing live ducks and living with them in his New York studio. He followed the ducks around on his hands and knees, drawing continually. McCloskey filled sketchbooks with "happy, sad, inquisitive, stretching, swimming, scratching, and sleeping ducks."[2] When discussing his drawings for the book, McCloskey said, "You more or less have to think like a duck, too, and it helps you. You think of being just as small as you can."[3] In his book are scenes from Boston. He traveled to Boston from New York to record authentically the state house, Beacon Hill, and, of course, the public gardens. His finished book attests to his belief that "no effort is too great to find out as much as possible about the things that you are drawing."[4] (See Figure 2.20 from *Make Way for Ducklings*.)

FIGURE 2.20. Robert McCloskey: *Make Way for Ducklings*. Lithographic crayon. "She taught them to walk in a line. ..."

Research Activities

Following are some sources and ideas for doing research. Some places and ideas may be new to you. Others may be right in your home but you may not have thought of them as research material before.

Using Your Library's Picture Collection

Librarians keep on file pictures that are available for checkout. The size of the file varies from library to library, but the picture collection may be an extensive resource that will enable you to locate just the photograph you need quickly. The pictures are cut from magazines and are filed alphabetically by subject. They may go back many years and may include illustrations as well as photos.

When you draw from a photograph, it is important to remember that a photo may distort the pose of a person or animal. It is wise to combine life drawings with drawings from photos. Check the accuracy of a photo before using it as a primary drawing reference by finding other photos of a similar subject or by drawing from life.

Making Your Own Picture File

Buy a supply of manila folders, label them by subject, and begin your own photograph collection. Ask friends to save old magazines for you. Visit library discard sales and garage sales to obtain old copies of magazines that have good photographs for research. Excellent material can be found in *Ranger Rick, National Geographic,* and *Our World.* Clip and file. As you accumulate drawings in your sketchbooks, you can integrate these, too, into your picture file. Filing the drawings under subject headings will make them easier to locate than flipping through your sketch-

books. Include incomplete as well as more developed drawings. Perhaps you have captured a child's hand motion or the strain on the neck of a dog when he jumps up for a stick. Any successful drawing fragment should be saved for future reference. This not only will save you time later when working on an assignment, but also can assure accuracy in your drawing when the subject you need isn't immediately available.

Places for Research

Zoos: Try to make the zoo of every new city you visit one of your stopping points. You may discover animals you have never drawn before or new environments to record. Even visiting the same zoo at different times of the day can provide new drawing experiences. Note at what times certain animals rest or at what times they are particularly active because they are waiting for a meal.

Humane Society: If you do not own a pet, your local humane society is a good place to draw domestic animals.

Pet Shops: This is another good source for drawing animals. Check with the owner first, and then take time to draw the rodents, birds, reptiles, and fish you might not be able to observe so closely anywhere else.

Aquariums: Large city aquariums are fascinating places and offer unusual drawing opportunities to record underwater environments and creatures. Some aquariums have trained seals or dolphins who perform for the public. While your family or friends enjoy the show, you can be recording the seal as he moves from pose to pose, as was the case for Figure 2.2.

Natural History Museums: These museums are real treasures, because they enable artists to make detailed studies of animals. You can record the quality of the fur, hair, the exact shape of a beak or claw, and other fine points. The animals are usually set up in their natural environment, which also can be helpful. If you are drawing the whole animal, be aware that the pose of a stuffed animal may be distorted. Other sources for drawing the animal should also be used.

SELF-ANALYSIS CHECKLIST

After completing the exercises in this chapter, it is important to take time to evaluate your drawings. Think about these questions: Which aspects of the exercises were difficult for you? Which activities produced the most satisfying results? In which areas do you think you need further practice? Do you think you can make continued progress through self-study or do you feel the need to take classes?

The Resources section for this chapter includes books for self-study in each of the areas on the self-analysis checklist. You may find it helpful to show your drawings to artists in your community to help you evaluate your need for further work. Remember, the work of improving your drawing is a never-ending process, and each assignment that you encounter in your careeer will pose new problems to solve. The following list of questions will help you determine where you are now and what direction to pursue with further drawing practice.

Vitality

Good illustrations are infused with life. The book illustrator's challenge is to maintain the spontaneity of sketches in the final art. Some artists, such as Marjot Zemach (see Figure 2.21 for her sketches for *The Judge*), have

FIGURE **2.21.** Margot Zemach: *The Judge* (Harve Zemach). Pen and ink sketches.

been particularly successful at this. Zemach made hundreds of preliminary drawings before chosing the final renditions of the characters in *The Judge,* yet each character looks as if he or she were created on the spot.

Questions:

1. Does my drawing feel dynamic or stationary?

2. Are my characters stiff or do they look as if they can really move around on the page?

3. Do my people and/or animals have a convincing quality that makes them feel real?

Composition

The composition of a page can focus the reader's attention on a particular action in the story. When planning the pages, the artist must consider the relationship between the two halves of a double-page spread and how one page visually leads the viewer to the next page. A page's composition can be used to reflect the mood of the story by creating tension or a sense of comfort. Julie Downing's illustration for pages four and five in *Hannah's Alaska* (Joanne Reiser) tells the viewer that something important is happening

(Reprinted by permission of Carnival Enterprises)

downstairs. (See Figure 2.22.) The following questions may be applied to the drawings you did of environments and to your interpretive drawings. Keep the questions in mind when you develop drawings into final art for your portfolio.

Questions:

1. Is my drawing harmonious? Are its individual parts integrated into a feeling of wholeness?

2. What part of my drawing do I want to bring to the viewer's attention? Have I created this focal point? If not, how can I change the composition of my drawing to draw attention to this area?

3. Is my drawing balanced? Are the visual elements equally distributed throughout the page? Have I chosen to employ imbalance in order to emphasize something in the narrative?

Perspective

Some of the basics of perspective are eye level, vanishing points, foreshortening, and size change. *Eye level* is the height from which the viewer sees a picture. Chris Van

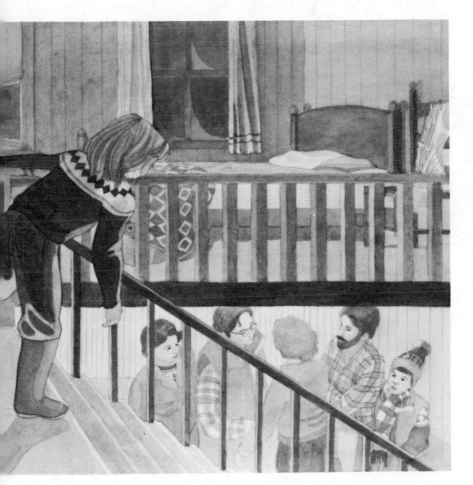

FIGURE **2.22.** Julie Downing: *Hannah's Alaska* (Joanne Reiser). Watercolor in full color. "'Somebody's down here!' my sister shouted. Emily and I hurried to dress and see who it was."

Allsburg's illustrations for *Jumangi* use dramatic changes of eye levels from one page to the next, which cause the viewer to observe details of his realistic pencil drawings. A *vanishing point* is the point in the distance of a drawing where the parallel lines of a drawing appear to converge. (See Figure 2.23.)

A drawing that has two vanishing points, such as an illustration of the corner of a building, is called *two-point perspective*, because parallel lines recede to each vanishing point. *Foreshortening* is the result of an object's receding into space. The part that goes into space appears smaller. As a figure

FIGURE 2.23. Nancy S. Hands. Pencil drawing with vanishing point.

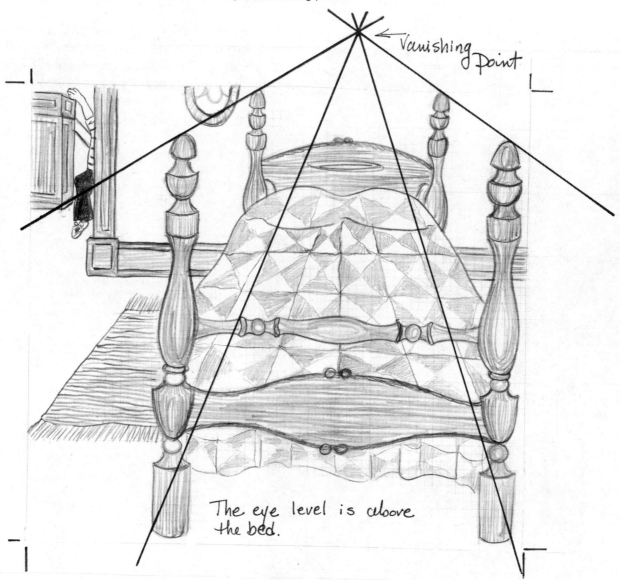

Vanishing Point

The eye level is above the bed.

or an object recedes into the background of a drawing it must be drawn in a size proportionate to its position on the picture plane.

Questions:

1. Have I determined the eye level and vanishing points in my drawing?
2. Have I changed the sizes of the figures and objects in my drawing according to where they are placed on the picture plane?
3. Is my use of perspective consistent in my whole drawing?

Anatomy

Knowledge of anatomy of humans and animals provides a basis for accurate drawing. A basic understanding of anatomy will help you complete drawings of children and animals in motion because you will be able to fill in missing parts when your subject has moved to another position. Even if your drawing is a simplification of a figure or a cartoon, the anatomy must be correct for it to be convincing, as in George Karn's little girl in Figure 2.12.

Questions:

1. Do I understand anatomical structure well enough to recognize when I have drawn part of a figure or animal incorrectly?
2. Can I fill in missing parts of a drawing when my subject has changed positions?

If you are just beginning the process of learning to draw, do not be discouraged by your inability to give affirmative answers to many of the preceding questions. These questions are meant to give direction to your future drawings. They provide specific goals to work toward if you are interested in directing your drawing toward children's books. If you find you have several areas to work on, you are not alone. Similar sentiments have been expressed by many of the artists whose work is printed in this book. The exercises in this chapter can be expanded upon and repeated with many variations. The more time you spend working at drawing, the more satisfying will be the results.

Looking at Artists at Work

FIGURE 3.1. Marcia Brown: *Once a Mouse*. Woodcut in two colors. "And tearing him from the crow's greedy beak..."

"People speak of some artists who use different techniques as if they had fifty up their sleeves ready to appear full blown when needed. But the life of an artist is one of constant preparation. He almost never feels he has realized his aim. When a book is finished, he usually is just beginning to feel how it might have been. Stacks of trial drawings attest to many efforts to find the right way to say what one has to say. One develops the technique necessary to express one's feelings about the particular book at hand."

MARCIA BROWN,
Horn Book magazine

USING THIS CHAPTER

Ten techniques will be explored in this chapter, including comments by artists who have successfully illustrated books using the mediums discussed. Although some of the artists offer specific advice for working in a particular medium, the focus of the discussions is not to teach you how to use a particular technique, but instead to extend the possibilities open to you through reading how other artists have approached working in a particular medium.

The chapter begins with a focus on older techniques. Many choices are available to modern artists because of improved printing methods, but brilliant colors can never replace expert use of black and white or sound draftsmanship. The artist beginning in the field usually starts with black-and-white and limited-color assignments. In this chapter, listen carefully to the voices of the artists, who know the value of working within limitations.

Each section describes one technique used by that artist. Before you read the chapter, turn to the lists of books illustrated by each artist at the end of each section. Check out of the library as many examples as you can, to refer to while you read this chapter. This will help you to study the work of the artists discussed in this chapter. The sections also list books illustrated by other artists using the same mediums. Look at some of these books to make comparisons of the use of the same medium. The Resources section cites books that explain in more detail some of the techniques discussed in the chapter.

As you read this chapter, keep in mind that the artist's most important criterion for selecting a technique must be the book's text. When an artist uses the same technique over and over again for each new text in the very same way, the art stops communicating and becomes a formula. The illustrator must delve into the heart of the text and bring out the mood, portray the setting, and show the uniqueness of the characters, instead of imposing an independent style on a text, suggests Leo Lionni. Lionni has likened a formalized style independent of the text to dressing the actors with the same costumes over and over no matter what the play is or what their roles are.[1]

Whatever the technique or style used in a book, it is important that the artist leave space for the child to interact with the book. This space, suggests Uri Shulevitz, is what engages the child's imagination. It means that the illustrator should evoke, rather than rigidly state.[2] Shulevitz's illustrations for *Dawn* (Figure 5.1) and *The Treasure* (Plate 9) are suggestive of a mood and give children room to make their own interpretations of the texts.

PRINTMAKERS

The three printmaking methods discussed in this chapter are forms of relief printing, where an image is transferred to paper from a raised, inked surface. Woodcuts date back to sixth-century China and came to be used commonly in European book illustration after paper was manufactured and moveable type was invented. The technique of wood engraving was refined by Albrecht Dürer in the sixteenth century and by Thomas Bewick in the eighteenth century.

Wood engravings are made from a piece of wood that has been sliced across the grain. This makes the grain stand on end. The artist can cut the block in any direction, using a sharp tool. This technique encourages small detail because of the closeness of the grain. (See the description of Thomas Bewick's work in chapter 9.)

The difference between a woodcut and a wood engraving is that in a woodcut, the artist must cut *with* the grain. The woodcut artist may also choose to employ the various effects of the grain's surface in an illustration. In a linoleum cut, the material to be cut is a special soft linoleum that the artist usually mounts on a block of wood for easier cutting and printing. Whether the material cut is end grain, softer wood, or linoleum, all three methods share a commonality in printing. The incised areas do not accept ink when ink is rolled over the surface of the block. The raised areas accept the ink when paper is pressed on top to receive the image.

Fritz Eichenberg: Wood Engraving

This book begins with a statement by Fritz Eichenberg that every book should be a thing of beauty, aimed at permanency. Mr. Eichenberg realized this philosophy in the many books he illustrated for both children and adults over a long and productive career. The statement, however, contains a paradox for his own work, because he can no longer obtain the kind of wood necessary to execute his wood engravings. Although the pieces he has created through engraving on end-grain Turkish boxwood have an enduring spirit that will never be erased, his favored method for illustrating cannot continue unless a suitable substitute can be found.

Fritz Eichenberg's love of wood and admiration of wood engraving came early in his life. He studied in Germany, where there was a long tradition of great wood printmakers, such as Dürer and Holbein. Wood engraving is a technique that demands complete involvement of the artist. As the wood responds to the engraving tool, the artist reacts to what is happening as he cuts the block. Fritz Eichenberg speaks of his personal relationship with each block of wood, where his tactile and emotional feelings enter into the process.[3] This makes the act of wood engraving much more than purely achieving technical competence. A study of the illustrations in the books listed will reveal his absorption in his work.

As Fritz Eichenberg works on a block, he creates "light, order, and beauty" out of the wood.[4] It is a slow process that permits no shortcuts and gives him time to think as he works. The block moves from darkness to light, bringing out the drama of a situation through his use of texture, light, and shadow. Figure 0.2 is an excellent example of a recent wood engraving, from Carl Sandburg's *Rainbows Are Made,* in which you can study these qualities that are typical of Eichenberg's work.

Fritz Eichenberg states that "the role of the illustrator induces you to slip into the skin of the people you are portraying. Your little block becomes a stage, you arrange the stage, the actors, and the lighting in order to express yours and the author's convictions."[5] His own conviction is evident in the way he marshals all the artistic elements to convey the message of the moment.

The process of wood engraving for Fritz Eichenberg begins with a pen-and-ink drawing that he transfers to a darkened wood block using carbon paper. He uses precisely sharpened gravers to bring light and drama to the wood. Some of the tools were given to him by his teachers in Germany, and he has continued this tradition by passing on tools to his students. Knowing where to stop, leaving dark areas, is one of the challenges of cutting a block. He finds it helpful to keep the mindset of a stage director when making decisions. When he thinks the block is complete, he pulls a proof print, using a smooth, slightly absorbent paper, matte ink, and a proofing press. The careful impression of ink on paper keeps the white lines open and the black lines sharp. He is in complete control of the end product, which can then be reproduced directly from his print.[6]

In the 1984 Arbuthnot lecture, Fritz Eichenberg made a statement that reflects the feelings of many of the best illustrators: "I committed myself to a certain quest for perfection in my work which I have not reached yet." His statement serves as an inspiration for each aspiring illustrator to pursue an education that "knows no beginning and no end."

Books illustrated by Fritz Eichenberg using the technique of wood engraving:

Dick Whittington and His Cat

Puss in Books

Rainbows Are Made (Carl Sandburg)

Mr. Eichenberg also used wood engravings in illustrating many adult classics. *Wuthering Heights* and *The Tales of Edgar Allen Poe* are two examples. A complete record of his wood engravings is found in *Wood and the Graver: The Art of Fritz Eichenberg*.

Books illustrated by other artists using wood engravings:

Thomas Bewick: *Select Fables of Aesop and Others*

George Cruikshank: *Collection of German Popular Stories* (Grimm)

Sir John Tenniel: *Alice's Adventures in Wonderland* (Lewis Carroll)

Gail E. Haley: Wood and Linoleum Cut

Gail Haley is a modern practitioner of the long printmaking tradition of book illustration. When she lived in England, she studied the wood engravings of Thomas Bewick and the German wood engravers. She has used traditional techniques imaginatively to create just the effect she desires to illustrate a particular text. The bold, classic feeling of wood and linoleum cuts appeals to her.

"In a computer age, I don't think children should see perfection in books. Instead, there should be room for children to move into a text."[7] Gail Haley strives to convey feeling in her work, rather than to achieve perfection. This concern for feeling gives her books a warmth to which children respond.

This does not mean, however, that she is unconcerned with detail or accuracy. Each of her books has been extensively researched with an attitude that reflects an uncompromising respect for children's intelligence and perception. She immerses herself in the culture of the story she has chosen to illustrate by studying the art, music, food, and life style of the people and times of the story. For *A Story–A Story*, her Caldecott Award-winning African folk tale, Gail Haley watched African dancers, visited museums, traveled to the Caribbean, and invited an African woman to live in her home. Many of the visual images in the book are modeled after African sculptures and artifacts. Her research process for *A Story–A Story; Go Away, Stay Away;* and *The Story of the Green Man* are carefully documented by Weston Woods in two excellent films: *Gail E. Haley: Wood and Linoleum Illustration* and *Tracing a Legend: The Story of the Green Man.*

Jack Jouett's Ride (see Plate 1) demonstrates how Gail Haley uses linoleum to achieve an effect similar to traditional wood engraving. She was interested in using the technique of wood engraving for the story because Jack Jouett was a contemporary of Thomas Bewick; yet she also wanted to work in a large format. Through experimentation, she discovered she could cut the linoleum with engraver's tools to achieve an effect very much like wood engraving.[8]

Gail Haley's method of printing also involves experimentation and results in a remarkable fidelity of the printed art to her original prints. (See Figure 3.2 for a picture of Gail Haley pulling proof from her press.) The black print is pulled separately and will become a separate negative when photographed by the printer. This results in a strong black outline. Next she prints the same lines using oil-base white ink on handmade Japanese rice paper. The white lines serve as a border in which she applies watercolors for the coloring of the prints. The watercolors achieve some random effects on the rice paper as they spread up to the white lines. The color work is sent to the printer, who makes the color separations that will then be combined with the strong black lines.[9]

Gail Haley's attitude toward her work demonstrates a willingness to spend whatever time and thought is necessary to illustrate a particular text. Her enthusiasm and patient research result in books that provide visual images that teach children about the world from which the stories derive.

FIGURE 3.2. Photograph of Gail E. Haley.

(Reprinted permission of Weston Woods)

**Books illustrated by Gail Haley
using wood or linoleum cut:**

A Story–A Story

Jack Jouett's Ride

Go Away, Stay Away

The Story of the Green Man

The Post Office Cat

**Other books illustrated with
wood or linoleum cuts:**

Marcia Brown: *All Butterflies; Dick Whittington and His Cat; How Hippo; Once a Mouse*

Ed Emberly: *Drummer Hoff* (Barbara Emberly)

Antonio Frasconi: *The Snow and the Sun; See and Say*

Clement Hurd: *Winter Birds* (Edith Hurd)

Evaline Ness: *Sam Bangs and Moonshine*

Compare the use of woodcut in several of these books. There is a diversity in the use of this method of illustration. Some artists make extensive use of the grain while others do not. The use of color is another good point of comparison.

If you are interested in other printmaking techniques not discussed in this chapter, you may look at books illustrated by the following artists:

Cardboard cut:

Blair Lent: *The Wave* (Margaret Hodges); *Oasis of the Stars* (Olga Economakis); *Pistachio*

Lithography:

James Daugherty: *Abraham Lincoln*

Ingri and Parin D'Aulaire: *Ola* and *The Terrible Trollbird*

Jean Charlot: *A Child's Goodnight Book* (Margaret Wise Brown)

Wanda Gag: *ABC Bunny*

Robert McCloskey: *Make Way for Ducklings*

BLACK AND WHITE TECHNIQUES

Ernest Shepard: Pen and Ink

The work of Ernest Shepard makes excellent study because of his use of pen and ink to create living characters that seem as if they could jump off the page. His work was never overdrawn, yet he used enough line to indicate the anatomy of a body and the essence of an expression. We feel he took time to know his characters so well that once we see them, it is hard to imagine them portrayed in any other way.

No other illustrator will ever dislodge Ernest Shepard's characterizations of Winnie the Pooh or Christopher Robin. His illustrations for the A. A. Milne books are rare examples of an artist's merging himself so completely with the writing that the visual images created feel too right to leave room for another artist to reinterpret them.

Shepard's style is strong and sure. Like the earlier English artist Caldecott, Shepard included just enough in a drawing to make it work. In Figure 3.3 from Kenneth Grahame's *Bertie's Escapade*, the animals look as if they are running across the page. The lines draw the viewer into the action. Each drawing contains just enough detail to create interest, never any more than is necessary. With the slightest stroke of the pen, Shepard could create an expression on an animal's face that

FIGURE 3.3. Ernest Shepard: *Bertie's Escapade* (Kenneth Grahame). Pen and ink.

makes the viewer empathize with the animal's predicament.

Perhaps the vitality in Ernest Shepard's pen-and-ink drawings attests to his continual drawing from life. He was a war artist during World War I and drew on the battlefield. In his studio he constantly drew from models. For the A. A. Milne books, he traveled to the places that were written about in the stories and captured those scenes in his sketches.

Shepard's characterizations in pen and-ink may be images that have remained with you since your own childhood. Perhaps you so readily accepted them you never stopped to analyze why you liked Pooh, Piglet, Eeyore, and the others. Now return to the books and look more closely at his strong lines, use of light and dark, feeling of action, and excellent draftsmanship. Your study should reveal why his work endures and remains well loved today.

Books illustrated by Ernest Shepard using pen and ink:

Bertie's Escapade (Kenneth Grahame)

The House at Pooh Corner (A. A. Milne)

Now We Are Six (A. A. Milne)

When We Were Very Young (A. A. Milne)

The Wind in the Willows (Kenneth Grahame)

Winnie the Pooh (A. A. Milne)

Books illustrated by other artists using pen and ink:

Erik Blegvad: *The Cat From Nowhere* (Monica Stirling)

Louis Darling: *Runaway Ralph* and *The Mouse and the Motorcycle* (Beverly Cleary)

Robert Lawson: *Ferdinand* and *Wee Gillis* (Munro Leaf)

Maurice Sendak: *Higglety Pigglety Pop!*

Uri Shulevitz: *The Magician*

Garth Williams: *Charlotte's Web* (E. B. White)

Scratchboard

Scratchboard, also called scraper board, is a specially manufactured board coated with a sized whiting or clay. Dense black ink is applied to its hard, smooth surface. The ink is scratched with a sharp tool in order to create a variety of effects. The result: clearly defined images that reproduce well and blend nicely with the typography of the printed page.

Leonard Everett Fisher: Scratchboard

Leonard Everett Fisher uses scratchboard to express the "drama, form, and clarity of visual reality."[10] The illustration from *The Death of the Evening Star* (see Figure 3.4) is characteristic of his use of dark and light to bring out the drama of the moment he has chosen to illustrate. Over the years he has created thousands of scratchboard drawings for children's books, and his work is distinguished by its graphic interest and impact.

Mr. Fisher's use of scratchboard as an illustrative medium evolved from a concern for rendering tonal form in paintings on egg tempera panels. His personal work was rooted in medieval Italian form drawings which eventually led to the use of scratchboard as another way to render form clearly. The forms of the people and objects in Leonard Everett Fisher's illustrations are depicted with a sureness that makes them convincing. He advises artists to make sure that they thoroughly understand the forms being rendered when using scratchboard. Because of the linear nature of the page, a form can only be an abstraction and must be clear in order to be understood.[11]

Although Leonard Everett Fisher has illustrated many books in scratchboard, he is foremost a painter. Recent works illustrated with acrylic paintings—*Seven Days of Creation* and *Sky Songs* (Myra C. Livingston)—reveal a different aspect of his art. Forms become more abstract. Children mull over the colors and images to bring their own interpretations and feelings to them.

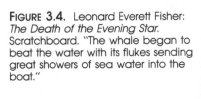

FIGURE 3.4. Leonard Everett Fisher: *The Death of the Evening Star.* Scratchboard. "The whale began to beat the water with its flukes sending great showers of sea water into the boat."

The style of these two mediums differs greatly, but a similar concern can be felt throughout Mr. Fisher's work. He wishes to portray the inner reality of a situation and to explore the essence of humanity through his art.[12] A close look at his illustrations shows a great concern for the inner life of the humans portrayed. This comes out in the intensity of their expressions, whether in a fictional work or a realistic account in an American history text.

Books illustrated by Leonard Everett Fisher using scratchboard:

Across the Sea From Galway

All Times All Peoples (Milton Meltzer)

The Death of the Evening Star

The Unions

A Russian Farewell

The Schoolmasters

Books illustrated by other artists using scratchboard:

Barbara Cooney: *Chanticleer and the Fox*

Don Freeman: *Beady Bear; Corduroy*

Stephen Gammell: Pencil

Stephen Gammell mines the capabilities of the pencil to create a wide range of moods. He evokes contemplative and mysterious feelings in *The Old Banjo*, while *Once Upon McDonald's Farm* is full of humor. (See Figure 3.5.) He feels that he draws best when he works with a text that allows him to interpret freely. Poetry is one form of writing that he feels especially suits his approach to illustrating. He prefers to create a setting for the text rather than to illuminate the words. This approach compels viewers to use their own imaginations when reading or looking at a book that Stephen Gammell has illustrated.

Pencil became Stephen Gammell's main tool of expression over the years. As other mediums fell away from use, he found himself concentrating on pencil. He advises new artists to choose their medium in a similar way. "New artists will find out if pencil will work for them or not. If it doesn't, they will go on to something else."[13] In two recent books that Stephen Gammell both wrote and illustrated, he used watercolor. In *Git Along Old Scudder*, he felt watercolor would convey the beauty of the scenery and colorfulness of the character. For *Wake Up Bear . . . It's Christmas*, watercolor shows the festiveness and warmth of Christmas.

This flexible attitude is revealed in the way Stephen Gammell approches his pencil drawings. He works on large-size fine drawing paper and constantly changes the drawing until he achieves the feeling he desires. This process may take several days' work on one drawing. If he is not satisfied with the result, he puts the drawing aside and begins again. The use of pencil allows him to make changes freely as his drawing evolves. He likes to emphasize the white space on the page to enhance the mood of an illustration. (See Figure 2.9 for an example of a landscape drawing.)

As Stephen Gammell looks back on his work, he sees ways he could have done things differently. He notes that while he has changed, the art in a printed book remains unchanged. He would like someday to be able to give new interpretations to some of his previous books. Although the printed art in his books remains fixed, his way of work-

FIGURE 3.5. Stephen Gammell: *Once Upon Old MacDonald's Farm*. Pencil sketch.

ing encourages children to bring their own interpretations to Stephen Gammell's work.

Books illustrated by Stephen Gammell using pencil:

The Best Way to Ripton (Maggie Davis)

The Old Banjo (Dennis Hasley)

Once Upon McDonald's Farm

Scary Stories to Tell in the Dark (Alvin Schwartz)

Waiting to Waltz (Cynthia Rylant)

Where the Buffaloes Begin (Olaf Baker)

Books illustrated by other artists using pencil or graphite:

Michael Deraney: *Yussel's Prayer* (Barbara Cohen)

Richard Egielski: *I Should Worry, I Should Care* (Miriam Chaikin)

Charles Mikolaycak: *Journey to the Bright Kingdom* (ElizabethWinthrop)

Ed Young: *The White Wave* (Diane Wolkstein)

Several other black and white techniques have been used to illustrate children's books. Many books have been beautifully illustrated in India ink wash with pen accents, such as Uri Shulevitz's illustrations for Isaac Bashevis Singer's *The Golem* and Tony Chen's work *In The Land of Small Dragon*. Another black and white technique that was more common in older books is dry brush and ink. This technique can be seen in Leonard Weisgard's illustrations for Washington Irving's *Rip Van Winkle*, Margot Zemach's *The Nose* (Harve Zemach), and Henry Pitz's rendition of *Treasure Island* (Robert Louis Stevenson).

LIMITED COLOR

The comments by Donald Carrick that follow introduce a technique that is routinely expected of illustrators. When two or three colors are used to illustrate a book, publishers expect artists to be able to prepare separate pieces of final art for each color to be printed. This hand-done method saves the high cost of photographic or laser-scan methods of color separation. In spite of the extra time it takes to prepare the art, some artists prefer working in this method because they have greater control over the results. The details of this method will be explained in chapter 7.

Donald Carrick: Hand Separations in Wash for Three-Color Art

Donald Carrick's watercolor illustrations are characterized by a quietness that invites children to linger over the pages and to think about the events in the stories. Many of the books he has illustrated were written by his wife, Carol, and together they have recreated everyday scenes and universal events that occur in the lives of children. The Carrick picture books invite children and adults to return to them over and over in shared moments together.

Most of the situations in the books that Donald Carrick illustrates call for natural flesh and earth tones. He has developed his own way of doing three-color separations to create the soft natural tones required in his books and has pushed what seems to be a confining technique to a high level. Donald Carrick writes that "perhaps the limitations are a comfort and create a oneness in the book."[14] A study of his books shows a wonderful harmony between the words and the moods and feelings he expresses in his water-colors.

There are limitations to three-color pre-separated art. Donald Carrick recognizes the possibility of overworking a drawing when it is repeated three times. (See Figures 7.10, 7.11, and 7.12 for examples of his final art prepared in black for green, yellow, and red photographic plates.) The color range is limited because only one tone of a color may be mixed with a second color, or black, to make other colors. He writes, "there is never the chance for the beautiful other color to make the page sing,"[15] as there is when using a full palette.

He suggests that artists doing color separations for the first time choose simple, compatible colors. First, use the colors as a decorative device, and then work up to a more complicated mix. He also advises artists to thoroughly understand the printing processes and terminology so that they can communicate precisely with their art director and printer. Artists should ask many questions of the printer in order to learn what the printer needs for the final art.[16]

Donald Carrick's method of working is to make a watercolor sketch for a page, using the colors in which the book is to be printed. (See Plates 2 and 3.) He uses a color chart to break the desired colors into percentages of value, in order to indicate the exact color for the printing inks and to use as a guide for translating into percentages of black for his final art. The little cutout squares show where a swatch has been taken out to match printer's colors. The final art is done on watercolor paper over a light box, using pencil and black ink washes in the correct percentages.

Although this technique is laborious, Donald Carrick's final illustrations do not lose vitality when printed. (See Plate 3 for the final art.) His illustrations remain loose and capture both the mood and action of the moment. The quiet tones gently invite the child reader to enter the world created in the books.

Books illustrated by Donald Carrick using three-color washes:

The Accident (Carol Carrick)

The Climb (Carol Carrick)

The Foundling (Carol Carrick)

Harald and the Giant Knight (Donald Carrick)

Lost in the Storm (Carol Carrick)

Patrick's Dinosaurs (Carol Carrick)

Books illustrated by other artists using three-color wash separations:

Arnold Lobel: *Frog and Toad* series; *Mouse Tales*

Maurice Sendak: *Little Bear* (Else Holmelund Minarik)

Uri Shulevitz: *Rain Rain Rivers*

A related method is used by artist Margot Tomes. She often illustrates in three colors, combining pen and ink for the black plate with tempera for the colors. Her use of tempera results in a less transparent overlay. Study her work in the unique biographies by Jean Fritz, *And Then What Happened, Paul Revere?* and *What's the Big Idea, Ben Franklin?*

FULL COLOR

Any method of illustrating that uses a full palette of colors is called full-color art. There are other full-color techniques that are not described in this chapter. A study of illustrated books attests to the ingenuity of artists in experimenting with many ways of working. Often it is difficult to tell just what the artist has used. Many full-color books are illustrated in combinations, such as watercolor and pencil. Sometimes what appears to be colored pencil may be brush and colored inks. Watercolors have been used in a variety of ways. Tempera and gouache are also used successfully. Your own favorite methods will lead to new discoveries as to what will work for you. Pay special attention to how artists handle their technique to convey just the right sense for a story. This type of analysis will give you practice in the kind of decision making you may someday face.

Charles Mikolaycak: Colored Pencil

"Pencil technique, like all art, must become one's own handwriting," writes Charles Mikolaycak.[17] Charles Mikolaycak has been developing since childhood his own way of drawing with colored pencils. He still enjoys the sound his pencils make on the illustration board.[18]

He offers important advice to new artists trying the medium: Select brand-name, high-quality pencils and experiment with different types to see which has the qualities you enjoy working with. Also, experiment with various paper surfaces and compare the results. He finds a good electric pencil sharpener a necessary tool.

Colored pencil work usually requires camera or laser scan separations. This means that when executing the final art, the pencil lines must be very fine and sharp in order to prevent blurring when reproduced. Keep in mind that the printing process will always make the printed version softer than the original art.

Charles Mikolaycak teaches a book il-

lustration/design course at Syracuse University and tells his students to "seek their own mind's eye visions."[19] He encourages students to develop their own uniqueness rather than to ape a style. This requires the student to go beyond learning how something is done, to add a new quality to their work. Such an approach may require much experimentation.

The experimental attitude that he suggests to his students is incorporated into his own work. He combines pencils with other mediums to solve particular illustrative problems. Watercolor or oil glazes may be applied over the penciled areas. Sometimes he works on colored paper. He is willing to experiment for as long as it takes to achieve the desired effect.

Many of Charles Mikolaycak's illustrations have been for folk tales from diverse cultures. A look at the stories he has illustrated reveals a variety of ways in which he has used graphite or colored pencils either alone or in combination with watercolor and glazes. The illustrations capture the drama of the moment. Often the composition is used to focus the viewer's attention on the essential action of the moment. His illustrations also show a concern for accuracy and detail. Of the many books he has illustrated in colored pencil, he is most pleased with *Peter and the Wolf* "because the brightness of the color transcends the pencil look so that the medium doesn't call attention to itself."[20] (See Plate 4 from *Peter and the Wolf*.)

Some other books illustrated by Charles Mikolaycak using colored pencil:

I Am Joseph (Barbara Cohen)

The Boy Who Tried to Cheat Death (Carole Kismaric)

A Child Is Born: The Christmas Story
(adapted by Elizabeth Winthrop)

Peter and the Wolf (Sergei Prokofiev)

Babushka: An Old Russian Folktale
(adapted by Charles Mikolaycak)

Books illustrated by other artists using colored pencil:

Nancy Carlson: *Harriet's Recital*

Susan Jeffers: *Stopping by Woods on a Snowy Evening* (Robert Frost)

Eve Rice: *Benny Bakes a Cake*

Many artists combine colored pencil or graphite and washes. The pencil gives definition to the forms, yet is softer than pen and ink.

Books combining pencil and washes:

Adrienne Adams: *The Day We Saw the Sun Come Up* (Alice Goudy)

Arnold Lobel: *Fables*

Barbara Cooney: Acrylics

Excellence marks Barbara Cooney's work, no matter what technique she chooses for a particular text. In recent years, she has illustrated several outstanding books using acrylics.

Richness of color, authenticity down to the last detail, a strong sense of place, and the creation of atmosphere are some of the characteristics of Barbara Cooney's work—whether she is using a limited or a full palette. No detail is too small to be correct, and a child may discover a wealth of information about the time and place of a story through her illustrations.

Ox-Cart Man (see Figure 1.1) is rich with the visual details of nineteenth-century New England life. When you look at the il-lustrations, you feel transported back to a time when families were self-sufficient and living in harmony with the changing seasons. The landscapes invite the viewer to enter in and walk along the country roads with the father as he travels to and from Portsmouth Market. There is room for the children to travel in and out of the pages, observing details such as a radiant sunset along the way. The depth in Barbara Cooney's illustrations compels children and adults to return to her books again and again to share new discoveries and feelings.

Ox-Cart Man is illustrated in full-color acrylics with some prismacolor pencils used for shading and accents. An acrylic gesso ground of titanium white is applied before the painting is begun. This gives her paintings a luminescence and clarity. The paintings are done the same size as the reproductions in order to minimize changes in production.

A look at Barbara Cooney's work over the years reveals that she often has experimented in order to achieve a desired effect. *Miss Rumphius*, for example, was painted on gesso-coated percale which was mounted onto illustration board. Acrylics were combined with colored pencil accents on top of the ground to create pages that radiate with a feeling of light. (See Plate 5.)

Barbara Cooney brings much more than technical mastery to her books. Her obvious involvement in and enjoyment of her work can be felt in the pages of her books. This feeling is catchy and reaches out to children, drawing them into her books.

Books illustrated by Barbara Cooney using acrylics:

Emma (Wendy Kesselman)

Holly and Ivy (Rumer Godden)

Miss Rumphius

Ox-Cart Man (Donald Hall)

Sky Songs (Myra C. Livingston)

Spirit Child (John Bierhorst, translator)

Books illustrated by other artists using acrylics:

Leonard Everett Fisher: *Seven Days of Creation; Celebrations*

Ezra Jack Keats: *Hi Cat; Goggles*

Nonny Hogrogian *One Fine Day*

Ezra Jack Keats: Collage

Collage is the cutting or tearing of shapes out of papers or cloth and gluing them down on a flat surface to create an illustration. Collage appeals naturally to young children because it is close to their own way of creating art through cutting and pasting colored papers. It also appeals to their tactile and visual senses. The use of collage as an illustrative medium was made possible by improved full-color printing methods which permitted accurate reproduction.

In 1963, Ezra Jack Keats won the Caldecott Medal for *The Snowy Day,* which brought attention to his superb use of collage. This was the first book that he illustrated with collage. It is illuminating to listen to his words about how the process of creating *The Snowy Day* evolved. In his Caldecott acceptance speech, Keats spoke about his process of inventing for the illustrations. He did not have a preconceived idea of how he would illustrate the book except that he wanted to add bits of patterned paper to supplement the paintings. (See Plate 6 from *The Snowy Day.*)

"As work progressed, one swatch of material suggested another, and before I realized it, each page was being handled in a style I had never worked · in before. . . . I worked and waited. Then quite unexpectedly I would come across just the appropriate material for the page I was working on."[21] "Oilcloth became the mother's dress, the snow texture was created by rolling white paint over wet inks, while snowflakes were made by cutting patterns into gum erasers which were later dipped in inks and stamped. New relationships and patterns were formed. . . . when the book was finished, I was somewhat startled to discover that my way of working had been transformed. I had wanted this book to be special. And in turn I was rewarded with a technique that I feel has great potential."[22]

For a wonderful glimpse of Ezra Jack Keats at work, Weston Woods's film, *Ezra Jack Keats,* shows him at work in his studio making illustrations for *A Letter to Amy.* In the film, we see how he marbleized papers, saved them, and later put them to use in order to create the perfect mood in books such as *In a Spring Garden* and *John Henry: An American Legend.* He also collected pieces of cloth and paper to draw upon when he wished to create a certain effect. We also see how he used the urban landscape that was part of his daily life, translating the shapes, patterns,and textures into pages of *A Letter to Amy* and other books.

As Ezra Jack Keats worked on his books, he began with a visual idea of what would happen. He then began to imagine the characters talking to one another, and the story began to grow. As the sketches developed and he placed characters in the scenes, the story continued to evolve. The drawings were placed on the walls of his studio so he could see the flow of the book and make necessary changes. He likened himself to a choreographer arranging a dance.[23]

Books illustrated by Ezra Jack Keats using collage:

In a Spring Garden (Richard Lewis, editor)

John Henry: An American Legend

A Letter to Amy

Peter's Chair

The Snowy Day

Whistle for Willie

Books illustrated by other artists using collage:

Eric Carle: *The Grouchy Ladybug; Scarecrow Clock* (George Mendoza); *The Very Hungry Caterpillar* and *Why Noah Chose the Dove* (Isaac Bashevis Singer)

Roger Duvoisin: *Beaver Pond*

Leo Lionni: *Frederick, Inch by Inch; Alexander and the Wind Up Mouse; The Biggest House in the World*

Margot Zemach: Pen and Colored Inks

Margot Zemach likes to illustrate with colored inks because the inks can be both brilliant and subtle. She often uses the inks of various colors in layers to brighten, darken, or mix colors. Her color work has a strength and richness that gives her illustrations depth. The ink paintings are done on either high-quality watercolor paper or illustration board. She likes to see the texture of the watercolor paper show through on the smooth paper on which books are printed.

"I used to think that I would reach a certain age and achieve an ultimate technique which would make it clear sailing and I'd then be able to say whatever I wanted effortlessly," writes Margot Zemach.[24] Now, she realizes that although she can use eight or ten colored inks in all kinds of ways, it is not enough. "There are always more things to learn, to be able to give every book a whole different life."[25]

Although Margot Zemach's style is easily recognizable, each book is a distinct response to a particular story and breathes with its own vitality. In *The Judge,* pastel coloring, the wallpaper pattern, and costumes make the courtroom comedy seem right out of a scene from a Molière play. (See Figure 2.21 for studies from *The Judge.*) In *Mazel and Schlimazel,* the heavy brush outlines and deeper colored inks feel just right for a story set in an Eastern European village. (See Plate 7.)

The vitality of Margot Zemach's illustrations makes her work unique among the many artists working in the field today. Her people and animals look as if they are moving on the pages. They look out at the viewer with expressions that seem to say "Why me?" or "I'm silly, am I not?" The lioness in Plate 7, a watercolor sketch for *Mazel and Schlimazel,* seems to be asking "Why is this happening to me?" Such definite attitudes conveyed by a twist of the mouth or a shrug of the shoulders on a Zemach character reach out to the viewer, who can't help but get involved in the story's action. The characters that Margot Zemach portrays make children laugh because children can recognize themselves or others.

Margot Zemach's illustrations have often accompanied retellings of folk tales. She believes it is important to bring to the artwork an authenticity of time, place, and people. She does much research in order to incorporate the feeling of the particular period and setting into the artwork for a story.

Books illustrated by Margot Zemach using colored inks:

Duffy and the Devil (Harve Zemach)

It Could Be Worse (Harve Zemach)

The Little Red Hen

The Judge (Harve Zemach)

Mazel and Schlimazel (Isaac Bashevis Singer)

Nail Soup (Harve Zemach)

For Margot Zemach's life story, the book *Self-Portrait: Margot Zemach* is an account of her life. The book may be found in the children's section of the library.

4

Types of
Children's Books

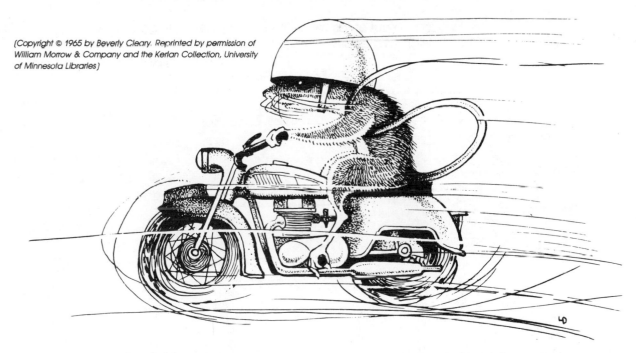

FIGURE 4.1. Louis Darling: *The Mouse and the Motorcycle* (Beverly Cleary). Pen and ink drawing for
chapter heading.

"Books don't go out of fashion with children; they only go out of fashion with adults."

MAURICE SENDAK,
Authors and Illustrators of Children's Books

USING THIS CHAPTER

There are many types of juvenile books that require illustrations. The purpose of this chapter is to acquaint you with some of the types of children's books, so that you can decide where your own art will best fit into the field. Although the picture book attracts artists because of the creativity it offers, it is unlikely that an artist beginning in the field will have the opportunity to illustrate a picture book. The following chapter will provide exercises for you to practice skills required for all types of books.

This chapter describes the special features of each category and suggests examples for you to look at to gain familiarity with the many types of books.

JUVENILE TRADE BOOKS

Juvenile trade books are the books that are found in retail bookstores and libraries. They are produced with an attention to quality of content, art, and printing, and in smaller numbers than other types of books. Popular trade books may have several editions, produced in different formats. For example, a successful picture book could have a retail cloth edition, a library edition with a different binding and cover, and a paperback edition.

Picture Book Format

A picture book can be defined as a book in which neither text nor art can stand alone. There are other books that are frequently called picture books, although they do not fit this precise definition. These books either rely totally on pictures to tell the story or have a story that can stand on its own without pictures. Following are descriptions of some of the types of books that follow the picture book format, although they are not picture books in the true definition of the term.

Wordless Books

As more and more books are being designed for babies and toddlers, the wordless book has gained in popularity. Children may use these books in family or classroom settings to stimulate conversation about the sequence of pictures. Figure 6.1 is from a page of Leo Lionni's *Who?*, showing a mouse greeting several animals. Young children can discuss who the characters are and imagine conversations between the animals. A one-year-old simply may name the animals, while the three-year-old may think of new conversations each time the book is used. *What?*, *Where?*, and *When?* are titles of other books in this wordless series.

Some wordless books are intended for children of an older age and are designed to stimulate creative thinking or to explore a concept through a series of connected visual images. Peter Spier's *Noah's Ark* encourages the child to retell the biblical story. Iela and Enzo Mari's *The Apple and the Moth* explores the life cycle of a caterpillar. Brinton Turkle's *Deep in the Forest* is a humorous reversal of the three bears' story. The books of Mitzumasa Anno cause children to stretch their imaginations in new directions. Mercer Mayer's wordless books delight through humor.

Exercise 1: Making a Wordless Dummy

An artist uses a dummy, or small sample book, to work out the visual concept for a story. You can begin to feel comfortable with this process by making your own wordless sequence stories, similar to a cartoon strip. Take a nine-by-twelve-inch piece of drawing paper. Cut it in half lengthwise and then fold each half into four sections. Tape the two halves together into a eight-frame sequence and use this to begin working on an idea for a wordless series of actions. Do not rely on words to explain anything that you do not explain in your drawings. Think of an idea that you can dramatize easily in eight frames. After doing one dummy, try several more. Perhaps you will come up with an idea that you will want to develop further. For excellent examples of clear visualizations, look at the examples mentioned.

Picture Story Books

In the picture story book the text can stand by itself. These books usually follow the same thirty-two-page format as the standard picture book, although some may be longer because there is often more text. Illustrated folk tales fall into this category. Folk tales make excellent stories for children's books because they contain universal emotions and events. The stories, passed down from generation to generation, have stood the test of time. They lend themselves to individual interpretations by artists. Many visually appealing books for children have been created from folk tales.

You may want to see the work of the following artists, who have illustrated many folk tales for children: Marcia Brown, Janina Domanska, Gail Haley, Charles Mikolaycak, Uri Shulevitz, and Margot Zemach.

Exercise 2: Making a Dummy for a Folk Tale

Fold and cut drawing paper into a small thirty-two-page book. Choose your favorite folk tale for the story line. Before you begin this exercise, find a folk tale that has been illustrated many times and see how the various illustrators have interpreted the same story. One of the Grimm or Andersen fairy tales would make a good choice. Think about how you would visually dramatize the story on the thirty-two pages of your dummy. Use pencil to make sketches that can easily be changed. Work on making one action lead to the next, creating interest on each page, and choosing the most meaningful actions in the story to illustrate.

Concept Books

Concept books explore a single subject or idea, often looking at the topic in a variety of ways. Toddler concept books follow an abbreviated format of the picture books, while concept books designed for four- to six-year-olds usually follow the thirty-two-page format.

Eric Carle specializes in creating concept books for children who are making the transition from home to school. His goal is to make this big change easier on the child by providing enjoyable books to teach new ideas that the child comes in contact with at school. The *Scarecrow Clock*, written by George Mendoza, introduces the concept of time using Carle's characteristic bright collages made with tissue paper that has been painted and glazed. (See Figure 4.2.) Eric

FIGURE 4.2. Eric Carle: *The Scarecrow Clock* (George Mendoza). Collage in full color.

Carle's popular *The Hungry Caterpillar* introduces the life cycle of the caterpillar to thousands of young children every year.

Good concept books may appear simple, but like the best picture books, they have depth through the way they approach their subject. The Carolrhoda *Start to Finish Books* take familiar objects in the child's environment and simply explain how they are processed. See Figure 4.3, *From Blossom to Honey*. The short text and bright watercolors explain the process of making honey succinctly and in a way that appeals to the young child.

Nonfiction Books

Nonfiction books for children cover a variety of subjects in the real world. Often they are written by people who specialize in certain subjects. If you have an area of expertise, you may want to gear some of your drawing to that subject. If you need a concise explanation about a topic, try the nonfiction section of the children's department at your local library. You will find many well-written and well-illustrated books that contain excellent drawings or photographs. There is a

FIGURE 4.3. Ali Mitgush: *From Blossom to Honey.* Watercolor in full color. "While the beekeeper takes out the frames, the bees buzz about excitedly."

wide selection of books designed to teach children about the world around them.

Illustrations for nonfiction books always must be accurate and well researched. This does not mean that they have to be dry or lacking in artistic appeal. The illustrations for *Labor Day,* by Cherie Wyman, are filled with life and are aesthetically pleasing. (See Figure 4.4.) Leonard Everett Fisher has made notable illustrations for many books, such as the Colonial America series. When you visit your library, look for David McCauley's *Cathedral* and *Underground,* and Edwin Tunis's *Colonial Craftsmen and the Beginnings of American Industry* and *Frontier Living.*

Photographs are also used to illustrate children's nonfiction. In chapter 6 of this book, the photographs of the printing process come from the children's book *The Puz-*

FIGURE 4.4. Cherie Wyman: *Labor Day* (Geoffrey Scott). Pen and ink in two colors. "Printers."

zle of Books by Michael Kehoe. Other books in this excellent Carolrhoda series explain such diverse and interesting subjects as how a road is made, the work of large-animal veterinarians, and how a pipe organ works.

Exercise 3: Explaining a Topic

Think about a topic you know a lot about. Maybe it is the herb garden on your windowsill, or perhaps the habits of cardinals. Do a series of drawings where you explain some aspect of the topic. For example, if you are an expert at growing herbs, you could show how they are planted, cared for, picked, and used in cooking. If you enjoy doing research, choose a topic you'd like to learn more about and make a series of drawings that explain an aspect of the topic that you think would interest children. Before beginning, decide the age level you are aiming for and keep your drawings simple or complex accordingly.

Biography

Biographies have grown richer in recent years as both writers and artists find ways to bring the events of peoples' lives to children. The accuracy called for in biographical illustrations does not preclude an imaginative approach. Margot Tomes's illustrations for the series of books written by Jean Fritz *(And Then What, Paul Revere?* and *What's the Big Idea, Ben Franklin?)* are excellent examples to study. Priscilla Kiedrowski portrays Ben Franklin in a lively characterization for *Ben Franklin's Glass Armonica* (Bryna Stevens). Figures 2.14 and 2.15 show two stages in her development of the character.

Easy Readers

Easy readers have gained popularity in recent years. These books are designed for children who are just beginning to read. Their format is that of a fiction book for older children, with chapters that give children the feeling that they are reading a grown-up book. In actuality, the amount of text in an easy reader may be no more than a picture book, but the chapter arrangement makes them seem longer. Chapters usually focus on one event that happens to the main character.

A standard format has been developed by the publishers for both the writing and illustrating of easy readers. The characters experience adventure and are often portrayed with humor. Plot is important, which gives an illustrator lively action to portray. Usually two or three colors are standard. The books are small in size.

Arnold Lobel's Frog and Toad books (see Figure 1.2) are easy readers at their best. He has stated that a children's book has to be many things at once: It should be graphically beautiful, both children and parents must enjoy it, and the book must appeal to all segments of society.[1] In the Frog and Toad books, the soft quality of three-color preseparated washes creates the intimate environment of his characters. Both children and parents love reading the books because they recognize themselves in the situations that Frog and Toad face. Both audiences also respond to the humor in the writing. The universality of these characters and their daily problems make them appealing to all people.

Other noteworthy easy readers are the Little Bear series, written by Else Holmelund Minarik and illustrated by Maurice Sendak, and Susan Pearson's *Molly Moves Out,* illustrated by Steven Kellogg. Some publishers have created nonfiction books in the easy reader format. Cherie Wyman's illustration for *Labor Day* (Figure 4.4) by Geoffrey Scott is part of a series that explains American holidays in a simple, interesting way for beginning readers.

Fiction for Older Children: 9–12 and Young Adult

Although Young Adult books are usually limited to cover illustrations, fiction for the nine- to twelve-year-old group may have from one to several illustrations per chapter. There are several formats for illustrated fiction. Some may have an illustration to begin each chapter. Figure 4.1 shows Louis Darling's illustration that begins Chapter 13 of Beverly Cleary's *The Mouse and the Motorcycle.* The illustrator included several spot illustrations for each chapter. The number of illustrations in each chapter may vary according to the actions the illustrator chooses to depict.

The editor may tell the artist how many illustrations to do, but it is the artist's responsibility to place them well and to portray the best actions or feelings. This requires the artist to read and understand all the subtleties of a book before deciding just what to illustrate. Some books require an emphasis on mood, such as Jim LaMarche's illustration for Emily Crofford's *A Matter of Pride.* (See Figure 2.18) Other books call for characterization, such as Ernest Shepard's illustrations of the animals in *Bertie's Escapades,* by Kenneth Grahame, (Figure 3.3). In *The Death of the Evening Star,* Leonard Everett Fisher emphasizes drama and action (Figure 3.4).

Most books illustrated for older children are done in black and white, with perhaps a cover illustration in color. Many of these books show how black and white can be just as effective as color. Since the writing for older children usually has strong characters, interesting action, and a definite sense of place, the illustrations are often realistic and detailed.

Exercise 4: Choosing Actions to Illustrate from a Fiction Book Written for Older Children

Find a book that you especially enjoy. Read the book several times from the perspective of a would-be illustrator. Make some notes about the essential actions of the story, what the characters look and feel like to you, and the details of the setting. Limit yourself to one illustration per chapter, and note what you would illustrate and how. Make pencil sketches for one or several actions from the story. Choose one of the sketches to develop into a finished illustration, using a black-and-white technique.

Poetry and Song

Poetry books for children are produced for several age levels and in several formats. Books for the young child follow the picture book format, taking one poem and illustrating it in the thirty-two-page format. Susan Jeffers' *Stopping by Woods on a Snowy Evening* explores some of the feelings of being surrounded by snow suggested by Robert Frost's poem. *The Judge* (Harve Zemach) is a humorous poem that offered space for Margot Zemach to build up the illustrations to a rollicking climax. Songs have also been put in the picture book format.

Peter Spier's *The Erie Canal* offers an excellent way to teach children about a period of history through authentic illustrations of the old New York State waterway.

Poetry anthologies for children offer wonderful opportunities for artists to do interpretive illustrations. Figure 4.5 is Peter E. Hanson's pen-and-ink drawing for a poem about being alone. The drawing (from *The Cat Walked Through the Casserole*, Pamela Espeland and Marilyn Waniek) reflects the child's contentment at having time alone on a swing. In Figure 0.2, Fritz Eichenberg's wood engraving loosely suggests some images from Sandburg's poem about elm trees at the end of winter.

Exercise 5: Interpreting a Poem

If you enjoy doing interpretive drawing, select several poems to illustrate. Work on sketches and then develop one or more of your drawings into a finished piece using a black-and-white technique.

FIGURE **4.5.** Peter E. Hanson: *The Cat Walked Through the Casserole and Other Poems* (Pamela Espelund and Marilyn Waniek). Pen and ink. "Alone."

MASS-MARKET BOOKS

Mass-market books are produced in larger numbers than trade books and are marketed at lower costs in order to be sold in greater quantities. They are sold in many types of retail outlets as well as in bookstores.

The idea of mass-marketing books for children is not new. John Newbery mass-produced books to reach many English children in the nineteenth century. Many Golden Books that began appearing on supermarket shelves in the 1940s are still popular today. Feodor Rojancovsky's *Tall Mother Goose* is one excellent example.

The quality of mass-marketed books varies. Recent trends have created many new books for the very young child. These books often have unusual formats, and many are based on the reader's interacting actively with the book in some way. For younger children, the book may also be a puzzle; older children may be able to choose endings for scenes in the books.

Board Books

Board books have become very popular for the youngest audiences. The pages of these books contain illustrations that are laminated onto cardboard and have a plastic coating. The cardboard pages make it easy for small fingers to turn them, and the coating allows the pages to be wiped clean. They are also designed to withstand biting and ripping. Board books may be bound in a traditional format or fold out like an accordian. Many are wordless or have a single word per page; other books have a simple phrase or sentence on each page.

Leo Lionni's *Who? What? When?* and *Where?* book series (see Figure 6.1) is an ex-ample of an artist of excellence applying his skills to this type of book. The collages have graphic appeal, and the arrangement of figures stimulates conversation with children who are acquiring language skills. Helen Oxenbury's books also are good examples of this genre. Her figures are simple yet they have warmth. The book *Family* shows one member of a family in relationship to the baby on each page. The illustrations show that the young child is obviously loved by each family member, and it is a very reassuring presentation that can also stimulate discussions between the child and the person reading the book.

Board books are printed in full color, usually with watercolor as the medium. There is a great variety in artistic merit, with some being sensitively drawn and beautifully colored while others are very brashly colored with the feel of an advertisement rather than a book for children.

Novelty Books

This is a category of books with unusual formats in which the goal is for the child to interact with the book in some way. Toy companies are now marketing books packaged with a stuffed character from the book. Many books are designed to emphasize play more than reading or looking.

The concept of a toy book dates back to nineteenth-century England, with the books printed by Edmund Evans. These books were called toy books because they were small in size and very decorative. Some of the novelty books today could be equally beautiful if the same care were taken in their production. *The Nutshell Library* by Maurice Sendak comes in a tiny decorative cardboard box and is an excellent example of how a novelty format can be well done. An early novelty book that is still enjoyed by children is Dorothy Kunhardt's *Pat the Bunny*. The drawings may seem outdated today, but children love the touching activities in the book, and its warmth endures.

There is certainly room for the creativity of new artists in producing quality novelty books. It is possible that this area of mass-market books will keep expanding, with every imaginable type of idea turned into a book.

Interactive Books for Older Children

The idea of the child's interacting with a book has now been developed in books for older children. Readers are given the choice of choosing their own endings for adventures, mysteries, and romances. Both the writing and art in these books follow a formula, and the possibilities may be plotted out using a computer.

HOME-MARKET BOOKS AND BOOK CLUBS

Home-marketed books are gaining in popularity. These books are sold through catalogs. Book clubs also purchase the rights to publish books and produce their own editions. In order to market the books at a reasonable price, the book club editions may use less expensive paper and bindings. Although these editions may not look as attractive or be as durable as the original book, they have the advantage of being accessible to more children. Companies who traditionally have made other products for children are moving into this field. One example is Johnson &

Johnson, who have added books for babies to their products. The Dr. Seuss "I Can Read" series has been marketed this way for many years. Schools also serve as a way to market book club editions through classroom book orders of special editions of books.

EDUCATIONAL PUBLISHING

Educational publishing is an area that you may wish to consider as a beginning source of free-lance work. Before contacting a company, check on their policy for hiring free-lancers, because many companies employ full-time staff artists. If you are unfamiliar with the artwork in educational books, take some time to familiarize yourself by visiting a school in your community and looking through the recent language arts, social studies, and science books. The quality of art in schoolbooks can be excellent. Often the art is in full color. An educational publisher may provide you with the opportunity to begin illustrating for children.

Exercise 6: Locating Educational Publishers in Your Community

Check the local yellow pages to see if there is an educational publisher within driving distance from your home. Many educational publishers are located in smaller communities, and you may be surprised to find several near your home. Write or call to find out their policy for using free-lance artists. Ask them to send you a catalog. Educational publishers have booths at state teachers' conventions. Find out when your state is holding a convention and go to collect catalogs of publishers. Once you have a professional portfolio, try seeking work from your closest educational publisher.

The Picture Book: Focusing on a Special Art Form

FIGURE 5.1. Uri Shulevitz: *Dawn*. Four-color wash done by hand separations. "And light a small fire."

"A picture book, like any other art form, has a life energy of its own. Take that away and all you have left is an empty shell. Therefore, why not treat a picture book with care in order to make it grow like a plant or animal?"

URI SHULEVITZ,
The Illustrator's Notebook

USING THIS CHAPTER

The picture book is a unique art form that requires a special way of visual thinking. It is economical in its use of words, yet it offers visual artists the chance to test their imaginations in a way no other book can. The term picture book has been used as a label for many types of books that are heavily illustrated. It is important to define "picture book" as it will be used in this chapter. A picture book is a harmonious marriage between words and pictures in which neither the text nor the art can stand on its own. The illustrator must find space within the words to bring a new dimension to the text. This means that the artist must absorb all the subtleties of the words in order to be able to add what is unspoken. Alone, the meaning of the words is not clear.

To illustrate a picture book is a goal of many illustrators because of the expressive freedom it offers artists. The picture book has its own special structure, and it is important for new artists to understand its uniqueness. The most successful picture books have been written and illustrated by individuals who have a special sensitivity to this art form. The key elements are explained in this chapter using a picture book that has been acknowledged as an outstanding example, *Where the Wild Things Are,* written and illustrated by Maurice Sendak. Obtain a copy of this book from library or bookstore to refer to when reading the chapter.

STRUCTURE OF A PICTURE BOOK

Uri Shulevitz writes and teaches about the life energy of a picture book and how this positive energy mirrors the child's own life force. This view of a picture book as a whole with all of its parts organically related is the perspective from which this chapter is written. One way to understand the structure of a picture book is to liken it to a tree. Just as all the parts of a tree grow from its core, so should every element of the picture book be an outgrowth of the book's central meaning and purpose. The picture book is so economical that any extraneous features lessen its impact. Artistic decisions must always arise from a holistic approach to the book's creation.

The roots of a tree are similar to depth in a picture book. We may not see the entire root system of a tree, but we know that it is there in order for the tree to survive. A child may not immediately understand the underlying meaning of a picture book, but it is the deeper level that motivates the child to return to the book time and time again. This depth is created by the author's and artist's ability to express a basic human emotion or universal truth. It gives the book a significance that goes beyond the literal events in the story.

The branches of a tree radiate out. In a similar way, the themes and artwork of a picture book can lead the child's sense of discovery and imagination in many directions.

Plot Structure

The plot of a picture book follows the same pattern as that of the adult short story or novel. It begins with a statement, introduces a conflict, builds up to a climax, and ends with a satisfying resolution. The picture book is a highly condensed version of this form. It focuses on one theme or explores one event. The artist can use the illustrations to heighten the child's involvement in the plot through adding humor or surprise. The monsters in *Where the Wild Things Are,* for example, turn out to be more humorous than scary.

Where the Wild Things Are opens with Max "making mischief of one kind or another," so he is sent to his room. He retreats from this conflict into a dream world where a forest grows in his bedroom and he sails away to the land of the wild things. The tension builds as Max joins the wild things in a rumpus. Suddenly, Max realizes that he misses home, and the action slows down as he makes a safe return to his own room. On the literal level, Sendak takes the child on an imaginary voyage filled with the unknown and then brings him back to his familiar place. The deeper level of the book explores the child's emotional needs to act out and escape yet to still feel acceptance. All aspects of the book's artistic elements mirror the mood and plot of the story. Illustrations grow in size with each page as the tension mounts and activity heightens. When the situation begins its resolution and the activity slows down, the illustrations grow smaller.

CONTENT

The content of a picture book often explores basic emotions such as security and acceptance. These themes help children define where they fit into the world around them. Good picture books present these themes in a comforting way. The illustrator can bring a new dimension to a theme by the unique way he or she visualizes the character or situation.

Within *Where the Wild Things Are,* the universal themes of needing to be loved, to dream, and to have adventures are evident. The art presents these subjects in a lively and reassuring manner. When Max returns to his room after his journey, he finds a warm dinner waiting for him. Maurice Sendak included a piece of cake in his illustration of the room upon Max's return. The piece of cake speaks directly to children of Max's mother's enduring love. (See Plate 8.) The child reader knows that Max is forgiven and experiences that satisfying emotion.

The need for adventure is explored through the use of fantasy in *Where the Wild Things Are.* Max sails away to another time and place, tames the wild things, and even gets to ride on the back of a wild thing. The success of the fantasy is that it feels convincing to children because in the end Sendak brings Max home to the reality of his own room. Max needed to get away, but he also needed to return. The best fantasy in books for young children will never take children too far from the world they understand. If the character is a talking bear or a frog, that character is believable because children see expressions, clothes, or actions similar to their own. Fantasy must be rooted in reality and follow an inner logic of its own.

ELEMENTS OF A PICTURE BOOK

This section describes the parts of a picture book and discusses the ways an artist can use the pictorial aspects of a book to extend the meaning of the words. The example of *Where the Wild Things Are* shows how Maurice Sendak used every pictorial element of the book to reflect the story's central themes and emotional content.

Book Jacket

The book jacket, which may also be called the dust cover, protects the book and attracts both the child and the adult buyer to the book. As a sales mechanism it must reflect the interior of the book and attract attention. The book jacket names the author and illustrator and may include titles of other books written by the author. The spine of the jacket carries the book's title, author/illustrator, and publisher. Some books do not have separate jackets, so the essential information and art are printed on the cover.

The layout and typography of the book jacket are usually determined by a book designer who is responsible for the format of the whole book. The artist may have suggestions for a book jacket which should be communicated to the editor. Some companies allow the artist to design his or her own covers or to work with the book designer on this important element of the book.

On the cover of *Where the Wild Things Are,* one of the wild things is asleep on the shore while a mysterious-looking boat sails toward the shore. The illustration creates a feeling of suspense. It poses the questions: "Who is in the boat?" and "Will the beast wake up, and what will happen if it does wake up?" The illustration makes the child want to open the book to find out what will happen.

End Papers

The end papers are the pages that are glued to the reverse sides of the book's cover. Artists often make effective use of the end papers to set the mood of the book by decorating them with a design motif taken from the illustrations. Murice Sendak used leaves from the home of the wild things to create end papers with a graphic quality that harmonizes with the interior of the book. Unfortunately, because of economic constraints, decorative end papers are not used frequently in contemporary books.

Front Matter

The front matter comprises the first four pages of the book. Page one is usually the half-title page. Originally, this page protected the book. The half-title page carries the title alone and may have an illustration that anticipates the story. Pages two and three show the full title. These pages must also state the author, illustrator, and publisher. Page four contains copyright information, the date of publication, and printing information. It may also include a dedication by the author and artist. This format is standard for the front matter of the book. Some books deviate from this format and condense the opening pages.

Although the text of the book does not begin until page five for the artist in the standard picture book format, the artist may use the front matter to keep the momentum going from the interest aroused by the cover and to further lead the child into the book. On the title pages of *Where the Wild Things Are,* Max is chasing two wild things. (See Figure 5.2.) The expressions and postures of the characters suggest the drama to be found within the story.

Another element that may be employed in the picture book format is the tailpiece. This is usually a small illustration without words that is a way of winding down the story. It may be merely decorative, as the sketch for Margot Zemach's tailpiece for *Mazel and Schlimazel* (see Figure 9.20), or it may explain something about the story, as does the illustration for *One Monday Morning.* (See Figure 1.3.)

Sequence of Pages

One challenge that the picture book presents to the artist is to create a natural flow from one page to the next. The actions portrayed must follow one another in logical sequence.

FIGURE 5.2. Maurice Sendak: *Where the Wild Things Are*. Title page illustrations done in tempera and pen and ink in full color.

Interest must be maintained throughout the sequence so that the child is motivated to turn from one page to the next. This type of visual thinking is similar to animating a movie or drawing cartoons. It requires a unique type of visualization that is different from drawing single images or doing spot drawings for actions in a longer book.

One way that Maurice Sendak paces *Where the Wild Things Are* is to build up the size of the pictures from page to page. At the same time, the activity increases until we come to the wordless rumpus scenes packed with action and totally filling double-page spreads. The action builds up gradually. There is never more than a child can absorb, yet each page shows something new happening. The strong expressions on Max's face that change on every page also lead the viewer on to the next scene because Max invites the viewer to find out what he is going to experience next. The result is a unified sequence of visual images.

Page Composition

Not only do the pages have to relate to one another, but each page must be interesting in itself. Illustrators often use the composition of a page to draw the child into the action of the moment. As the artist plans the composition of an individual page, he or she must always keep in mind how it fits into the whole sequence.

Maurice Sendak has spoken about how he approaches each picture page. He considers the making of a page to be similar to the construction of a stage setting.[1] He builds up each element on the page to create a feeling of depth and place. In the illustration for Plate 8, our eyes are led into the space through the angles on the door, shutters, bed, and tail, to bring us to the table and its reassuring contents. The setting looks like a real room and needs no further embellishments. Sendak has used the composition of the page to create a feeling of intimacy in the space inhabited by Max. This invites other children to share in Max's experiences.

Whatever compositional devices are used by an artist, they are most effective when they do not call attention to themselves but harmonize with the natural flow of the story. The illustrator must decide the type of treatment to give a book, based on the story, and stick to that decision consistently. A folk tale from an older culture may suggest a two-dimensional treatment of space, as in Marcia Brown's *Once a Mouse.* (See Figure 3.1.) Uri Shulevitz finds it helpful to conceive of each page as a three-dimensional cube.[2] He considers where to place each object in relation to the picture plane. In his illustration for *The Treasure* (see Plate 9), we feel that Isaac has come from a distance and is walking toward us. The placement of the figure in the landscapes throughout the book draws the child into Isaac's travels.

Color

An illustrator must develop the ability to maximize the use of color in a book. Black-and-white or limited-color illustrations may be just as dynamic to a child as a book with bright colors. Detailed pen drawings, textured lithographic crayon, or soft pencil tones can be used to create interest or portray the mood of a story. Economic restraints have put a limitation on full-color printing, but artists should impose their own color limitations in response to the text. In *Where the Wild Things Are,* soft, muted pastel hues mirror the dreamlike quality of the story.

The artist has listened to the story in order to make color choices.

ACTIVITIES

Exercise 1: Making a Sequence Story

A picture book requires the artist to be able to tell a story through a series of visual images. These images must logically follow one another in order to be able to be clearly understood by the child. They must be varied enough to maintain interest in the story and motivate the child to turn each page.

You can practice the process of telling a story through a series of visual images by making your own sequence story. Try doing many of these in order to develop your skill. Begin by thinking of one simple action of a character. Then think about how you can translate the action into a series of drawings. In the action, include some obstacle to overcome or a simple conflict. End the sequence of images with a resolution of the situation.

Follow the same instructions as in Exercise 1 in the preceding chapter for preparing a small dummy. Your drawings will be small, quick sketches. Once you have chosen an event to develop, start drawing the sequence of events as you imagine them to happen. As you do your drawings, always ask yourself what logically comes next, so that the sequence is clear. (See Figure 5.3.) Keep the drawings and the idea simple. Try this process several times with different ideas until you feel comfortable about your ability to dramatize an event through a series of drawings.

FIGURE 5.3. Nancy S. Hands. Eight framed sequence story.

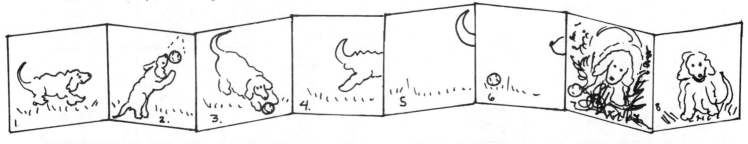

Expanding a Sequence Story into the Picture Book Format

Exercise 2: Preparing a Story Board

Many artists use a story board in order to visualize the whole concept of a book. A story board can be made from a large piece of drawing paper or an illustration board that is divided into enough squares to lay out an entire book. In the standard picture book format, an artist has twenty-eight pages in which to tell the story. Books are usually thirty-two pages long, with the first four pages taken up by the front matter. Some picture books are longer, but we will use the standard format for practice.

In this exercise you will expand one of your eight-frame sequence stories into twenty-eight frames. Take a large sheet of drawing paper and divide it into thirty-two frames that are not bigger than three-by-three inches. Keep the squares small so that you can concentrate on the flow of action rather than on detailed drawings. Choose the sequence story from the first exercise that you feel is most successful and that you feel you can expand into a complete story. (See Figure 5.4).

If you are not satisfied with one of your previous ideas, choose a favorite folk tale or a story that you like and work on visualizing your own images for it. Do not spend time at this point trying to come up with the perfect picture book idea. Your primary task is to experience the process of visualizing a whole story. Pick a story that will be fun for you to illustrate and that sparks your imagination.

When you have chosen your story, spend time thinking about how you can continue to develop it through sequential images. Keep in mind several goals: maintaining interest in the story, dramatizing the action, making one frame logically follow the next, and overall balance and impact.

In looking at picture books, you have

FIGURE 5.4. Nancy S. Hands. Story board with twenty-eight frames.

FIGURE 5.5. Don Freeman: *Dandelion*. First thumbnail dummy.

probably noticed that there are many formats. Some books have an illustrtion on one page with the text opposite. Other books integrate type and art on the same page. Some pages that face one another have illustrations that are separate entities; others have one illustration that flows over two pages. Two pages that face one another and share a drawing are called a double-page spread. At this point do not worry about the words, but keep in mind that eventually text will have to be placed into the book. If preparing a story board seems very difficult, return to some of the books listed in the Resources section and study how other artists developed their stories pictorially.

Exercise 3: Preparing a Dummy

The term *dummy* is used to designate a sample book that an artist uses to work out a complete concept for a book. A dummy is shown to an editor to indicate how the artist would illustrate an entire book. Some artists may not make a story board but may work directly on a dummy. Learning to make a dummy is essential for illustrating any type of book.

Some artists may begin with a small-size dummy, called a thumbnail dummy, which is the first working out of the entire book. Figure 5.5 is an example of Don Freeman's first tiny sketches for *Dandelion*. If you turn to the printed book, you can see how he had the character well developed even in this preliminary stage. Figure 5.6 is from a pencil dummy for page twenty-seven of *Lost in the Storm* (Carol Carrick). It shows Don Carrick's first small drawing for that page.

For this activity, practice making a dummy that is the exact dimension of the final printed book. Develop your drawings and indicate where text will be placed. First, consider the size of the book. If your story deals with intimate feelings and is for very young children, a small size is appropriate. Next, think about whether the book should have a vertical or a horizontal emphasis. If the illustrations are filled with landscapes,

for example, a horizontal format is appropriate. Whatever format decisions you make should be based on the content and emotional feeling of the story.

Although you are not writing a story for this exercise, it is important to practice fitting the text into your concept for the illustration. In many cases editors and book designers make format decisions, and the artist does not choose text placement. For this exercise, you will make this decision so that you can practice designing the entire book. Whatever format you choose for placing the words, one requirement must always be met: The words must be clearly readable. Many books have been ruined by printing words on

FIGURE 5.6. Donald Carrick: *Lost in the Storm*. Pencil dummy sketch.

> Grandma stopped spooning plum jam into the center of the sweet smelling pieces of dough. She moved closer to the window so that she could hear her grandchildren's conversation.

FIGURE 5.7. Nancy S. Hands: *The Best Thing About Grandma's Farm*. A dummy sketch.

too dark a background or over a brightly patterned background. The words must not be in conflict with the art in any way. See Figure 5.7 for a sample dummy with placement of text.

Make your dummy out of inexpensive drawing paper cut to the dimensions you have chosen. You can fold the paper to form a thirty-two-page book. Remember that the story does not begin until page five. After you have worked out the illustrations for your story, you can add appropriate drawings for the front matter. As you begin to transfer your drawings from the story board to the dummy, make changes that are needed and start to develop more detail in the drawings. The drawings should be complete enough to indicate your concept for the page and the whole book, but they do not have to be perfect.

Use pencil so that you can make changes easily. You may later return to your drawings and choose several pages from your dummy to develop for final drawings for your portfolio. Repeat this process with several stories.

Understanding Printing

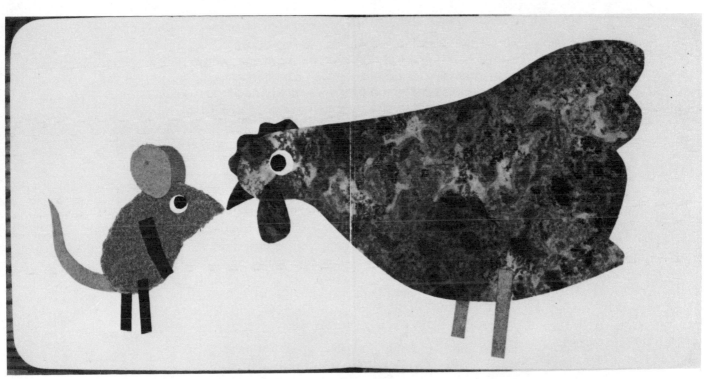

FIGURE 6.1. Leo Lionni: *Who? Pictures to Talk About.* Collage in full color.

"The kind of care that is taken in printing books is, I believe, very important. Children must grow up with a sense of quality, of excellence. To have little respect for our materials and for the things we make means to have little respect for the people for whom these things are meant."

LEO LIONNI,
Authors and Illustrators of Children's Books

USING THIS CHAPTER

The children's book artist must have a thorough understanding of basic printing terminology and processes. This is important for making the best choices when preparing art for print. Each decision has an effect on the printed product. The artist must know how to work within the limitations imposed by printing technology. Good printers take time to skillfully handle their tools to help the printed art achieve the closest possible facsimile to the original, but printers can only work within the capabilities of their equipment. Artists must know when they prepare final art how a camera tends to compress tones or has difficulty picking up certain colors.

Before you read this chapter, turn to the Glossary and read over the printing terminology. These words will be used throughout chapters 6 and 7 and should become part of your vocabulary in order to communicate effectively with printers and art directors.

Next look at the diagram of the roles of key people in the production of a book. (See Figure 6.2.) The diagram shows how all the personnel work together in order to produce a book.

After reading this chapter, visit a printer in your community. Firsthand observation of the production departments and the presses in action will strengthen your understanding of the printing process. Your visit will enable you to ask questions of the people involved.

Your knowledge of printing will be re-

FIGURE 6.2. Key roles in the production of a children's book.

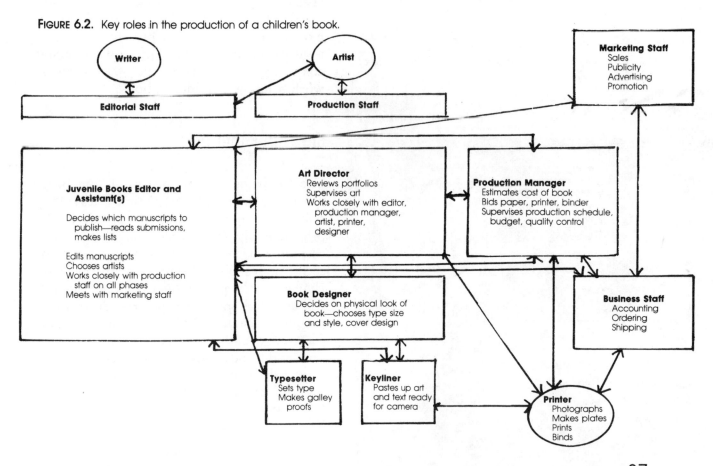

warded when it is time for you to prepare a portfolio or final art for your first assignment. You will know how to choose materials that will reproduce well. Editors who may have some hesitation in working with a new artist will be reassured when they know you understand the printing process.

OFFSET PRINTING

Offset printing is used almost universally for printing modern books. The term *offset* is a shortening of the full name: photographic offset lithography. A definition of each of these words explains what offset printing is. *Photographic* refers to the fact that the printing plates are made through photography. *Offset* is the way the image to be printed is trans-

ferred to a rubber blanket before it is transferred to the printing paper. *Lithography* is the process of sensitizing the plates based on the fact that grease and water do not mix.

Commercial lithography has been improved continually since the invention of lithography by the Austrian printer Senefelder in 1798. Senefelder discovered that when he drew on a piece of limestone with a greasy crayon and then sponged the stone with an acid mixture, he could create an image area that would accept ink and repel water. The nonimage area accepted water and repelled ink. When paper was applied to the stone under pressure, the image was transferred to the paper. In today's commericial presses, aluminum has replaced stone and the plates are sensitized through photochemical means. Speedy modern platemaking processes and presses have made offset lithography the most economical way to produce large editions of books in both black and white and color. Figure 6.3 shows an offset press at work printing a children's book.

Steps in Printing

The following description details the progress of the final art from the time it leaves the publishing company until it appears in the printed book. Procedures vary from printer to printer depending on what type of equipment is available. Computers are bringing changes to the printing field, and as technology advances some of these procedures are in a state of change. What is most important for you to understand is the general procedure and to be aware that changes are occurring. Talk to professionals involved in printing and skim through trade magazines to keep informed of recent developments.

FIGURE **6.3.** An offset lithographic press at work from *The Puzzle of Books* by Michael Kehoe.

(Reprinted by permission of Carolrhoda Books, Inc.)

(Reprinted by permission of Carolrhoda Books, Inc.)

FIGURE 6.4. Copy camera shooting original artwork. *The Puzzle of Books* by Michael Kehoe.

Several graphic arts magazines are suggested in the Resources section for this chapter.

Black and White Art

Camera Room: The first stop at the printers is the camera room. Special large copy cameras shoot the final art. (See Figure 6.4.) A high-contrast lithography film is used. The negatives are developed in a film-processing machine, and then they are carefully examined to make sure that the details are sharp and clear. (See Figure 6.5.)

Photographing Line Art: Line art is the simplest to reproduce because a film can be made directly from the finished art and transferred to the printing plate. *Line art* is the term given to a piece of art in which all tones are of equal value. The tones may be created through lines (as in cross-hatching), dots (as in stippling), or through larger solid shapes. Artists use line art to create the effect of tonality through the way they manipulate areas of black and white. Some examples of line art in this book are figures 2.1, 2.19, 3.3, and 4.1.

Photographing Tonal Art: Tonal art cannot be photographed and made into a printing plate without an additional step because the printing plate only reproduces from solid shapes. This means that a shade of gray must be converted into hundreds of tiny dots before it can be reproduced. The camera person places a ruled-line screen between the camera lens and the film. The line screen converts the tonality into thousands of tiny dots for the film. These dots are so small and close to-

gether that our eyes read them as a continuous tone. Newspaper photographs appear coarse because there are fewer dots per square inch than in a children's book or magazine reproduction. If you take a strong magnifying glass and examine dot patterns in a newspaper, you will see how the dots that are smallest and closest together produce dark tones while the dots that are larger and far apart produce light tones. Figures 2.20, 3.5, and 2.9 are examples of *halftone* art.

Color Printing

Color Separations: If the artwork for a book is to be printed in color, additional preparatory work is necessary before the printing plates can be made. Each color must have its own separate printing plate. In order to make the printing plate, a separate film must be made for each color to be printed. There

FIGURE 6.5. Camera man examining the negatives to make sure that they will reproduce well. *The Puzzle of Books* by Michael Kehoe.

(Reprinted by permission of Carolrhoda Books, Inc.)

are two ways the colors may be separated: by the artist or by machine. The work of the artist in separating colors will be discussed in the following chapter.

Until recently, it was the camera that did machine color separations, but now lasers are being used. This is an example of an aspect of printing technology in a state of change. Both processes are based on similar principles, but the laser has the advantage of being faster, which translates into a saving of money.

Full-color printing relies on the combination of the three primary colors plus black to achieve a complete spectrum of colors. These colors are called process colors and have special shades for reproduction purposes. Red is magenta, yellow is lemon yellow, and blue is cyan. (See Plate 11.) Black is added to these primaries to give form and definition to the art. What the camera or laser must do is to take a piece of full-color art and convert it to thousands of tiny dots for each separate process color. In camera separation, the camera person uses a special filter placed at a particular angle over the camera lens to block out all unwanted colors. The dot patterns on the film negative are examined closely, and color corrections are made by enlarging or decreasing dots. *Prepress color proofs* can be made, to check color accuracy, by running each color singly and then in combination on a small proofing press. This procedure is being used less often because of the improvements in laser scanning and the time and cost efficiency of the new technology.

Laser-scan color separations may not be done at the printing company but are often made at a business that specializes in this process. This means that full-color illustrations may require an additional step once they leave the publishing house. At the laser scanner, the art is wrapped around a transparent drum that allows light to pass through it. A laser-scan operator uses a keyboard to feed color information into the scanner. (See Figure 6.6.) Inside the scanner, numerical values are assigned to the colors that generate dot patterns at tremendous speeds. In a short time, a film negative emerges for each process color, containing the correct dot patterns. The film is then placed in a developer and inspected. Color proofs are made through a color match system, such as the *chromalin*, or through a color key system. These proofing systems have a great advantage over running proofs on a proofing press, because they are much faster. Chromalins are made from separate pieces of acetate, each accepting a dust of one of the process colors or black. Next, the four sheets are laminated together precisely one on top of the other. The resulting proof

FIGURE 6.6. Photograph of a laser scanner making color separations.

(Photograph courtesy of James Rekow and Color House, Inc.)

FIGURE 6.7. The stripper places the negatives in the correct position to form the pages of the book. *The Puzzle of Books* by Michael Kehoe.

should look exactly like the page to be printed except that its surface is glossy. The art director and editor inspect the chromalins carefully, and if the colors are not accurate, then the laser scanning may have to be redone.

Stripping and Imposition

Once the film negatives have been made, whether they are black and white or color, they must be positioned correctly for the pages in the book to be in the right order. The printing plates carry groups of pages in multiples of four on one plate. For many picture books, sixteen pages are grouped on one plate. The particular arrangement of pages is called imposition and is determined by the type of binding and color layout. The process of placing the negatives in their proper order is called *stripping*. The stripper cuts windows in sheets of sturdy orange vinyl that allow the negatives to show through. (See Figure 6.7.) The whole sheet is then put into a proofing machine and a *blueprint* or *silverprint* is made. The proofs are then cut up into a dummy book, so that the editor and production manager can check to make sure each page is in its correct place and the type and art on each page is accurately placed. Once the proofs have been approved, then the plastic sheets, known as *flats,* can be made into printing plates.

Platemaking

The platemaker takes the flats and places them into a machine with a chemically treated piece of aluminum. (See Figure 6.8.) Inside the machine a strong light sensitizes the aluminum so that the image areas will accept printing ink. The plates are put into a developer, washed, and dried. The result is a flexible printing plate ready to be wrapped around the roller of the printing press. The area that will print the image has been treated to accept ink and repel water, while the nonimage-carrying area has been treated

FIGURE 6.8. The photographic images have been transferred to an aluminum plate. *The Puzzle of Books* by Michael Kehoe.

to accept water and repel ink. All tones have been converted into tiny dots, and a separate printing plate has been made for each color to be printed. When fastened to the press, each plate will fall directly on top of the next so all colors will be printed in perfect *registration*, or exact alignment.

On Press

There is a variety of printing equipment available, and the type of press used for a particular book depends on the number of colors, the amount of books to be printed, and the presses that are free at the time the book is to be printed. A four-color book, for example, may be printed on a two-color

press with two passes through, or on a four-color press with one pass through the press.

Whichever type of press is used, all offset presses work on the same principle. The closeup of the plate-carrying area of the offset press in Figure 6.9 illustrates how they work. The printing plate is attached to the top roller and first passes through a dampening system. Next, it passes though ink rollers and then rolls onto a rubber blanket. The inked image area transfers to the rubber blanket. From the blanket the image is printed onto paper running through the impression cylinder below.

The rubber blanket is used because it is durable, does not wear the printing plates, requires less water contact with paper than other materials (a factor that reduces the

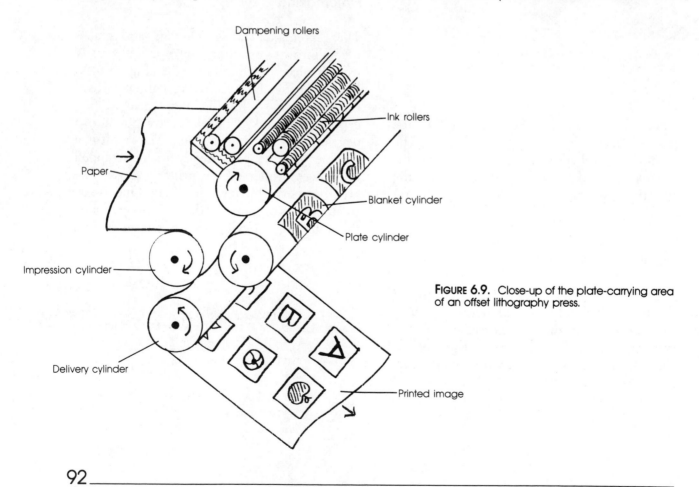

FIGURE 6.9. Close-up of the plate-carrying area of an offset lithography press.

FIGURE 6.10. The production manager from Raintree publications examines a press sheet and compares it to the chromalin proofs for accuracy of color and registration.

(Photograph by Nancy S. Hands)

negative effects of shrinkage), and allows finely detailed art to be printed on textured paper.

Rotary presses are used because of their speed. In the printing business, speed is always equated with economy. The faster one job can get off the press, the sooner another can take its place. This is a major reason why black-and-white art is less expensive to print than color. Each color requires more time in the prepress and press stages, multiplying costs accordingly.

Once the plates are on the press, the printer must check for color fidelity, even ink flow, and registration of the plates. *Color bars* appear at the top of a press sheet before it is cut and trimmed. (See Plate 10.) The printer uses the color bars to check these conditions. Before the full run is given the go-ahead, the printer and the production manager or art director inspect the press sheets carefully. They compare them to the proofs. Some adjustments of ink may need to be made. When the first sheets look fine, the go-ahead is given to print the full run. (See Figure 6.10 of a production manager checking the first press sheets by comparing them to the chromalins.)

Press Sheets: The production manager determines the size of the press sheets and the layout of the book well before the book goes into production. The *trim size* of the pages, type of press to be used, and bindery requirements are considered before choosing the printing paper size. The *imposition* of the pages, which the stripper has to follow so carefully, reflects all these considerations.

Imposition has a direct effect on limitations that may be given the artist in preparing art for a book. Many picture books are printed with alternating color and black-and-white double-page spreads. This is an economical feature that takes advantage of the fact that a press sheet can pass through the press and receive black ink only on one side, and, in the second pass-through, receive one or more colors on the second side of the sheet.

Exercise 1: Folding a Sixteen-Page Book with Alternating Color and Black-and-White Double-Page Spreads

This exercise will help you to understand how a press sheet is designed and cut into pages before being bound.

1. Take a piece of typing paper and fold it into eight equal parts.

8	9	12	5
1	16	13	4

6	11	16	7
3	14	15	2

FIGURE 6.11. Sample book imposition. Number the pages accordingly.

2. Number the pages according to Figure 6.11.

3. Take a colored pencil and mark each page on the front side to indicate that it will be printed in color.

4. Fold the page in half widthwise, so that no. 1 falls on top of no. 3.

5. Fold in half from the top down so that no. 5 and no. 6 come under next.

6. Fold the last half, bringing it underneath the other folds.

7. Cut the folds.

You should have a sixteen-page book with color indicated for every other double-page spread.

The press sheets are the first sign that the production of a book is drawing to an end. Figure 6.12 shows a press sheet coming off the press. Figure 6.13 is a photograph of the press sheet for *Clues in the Desert*, showing one entire signature of sixteen pages. As the press sheets come off the press they are stacked and ready for the next step, the bindery.

The Bindery

The bindery is the last step for the books before they are completed. Some publishers and printers operate their own binderies, while others send the books to a separate facility. When the press sheets reach the binders, they are folded and gathered into signatures. *Sig-*

FIGURE 6.12. A press sheet is coming off an offset press. *The Puzzle of Books* by Michael Kehoe.

(Reprinted by permission of Carolrhoda Books, Inc.)

FIGURE 6.13. Julie Downing: *Clues in the Desert* (Emmet Davis). Close-up photograph of the press sheet. The press sheet carries half of the book's thirty-two pages.

natures are the groups of pages that were printed on the same press sheet. Each signature is cut into individual pages (called folios) and then sewn together. The sample book you made for Exercise 1 contained two signatures. After the signatures are folded and cut, the excess paper around the edges must be trimmed off so that the pages are the correct size. Figure 6.14 shows the folding machine preparing to fold each sheet.

Different kinds of bindings are used, depending on whether the book is going to be in a bookstore, school, or library. School and library editions are bound for extra durability. Sometimes extra pages are bound into the front and back. These books are *side*

FIGURE 6.14. A folding machine at the bindery folds the pages of a children's book. *The Puzzle of Books* by Michael Kehoe.

sewn, which makes it harder to open them flat but is a more durable type of binding because the thread passes through the entire book at once. *Smyth sewing* is used for the bookstore editions. In this type of binding, the thread passes through each signature separately. Paperback editions are *perfect bound,* using adhesives rather than thread. This least durable binding often causes paperbacks to fall apart.

Once the books are trimmed, they are ready to receive a cover. (See Figure 6.15.) This process is called *casing in.* A binding material, which may be cloth or synthetic, is wrapped around heavy cardboard. An illustration may be printed on the cover of the book and run in a separate press run on a special kind of plasticized paper. The cover may also be plain cloth, with an illustration only on the dust jacket. Some books have a metal foil motif taken from the artwork stamped on the cover. Once the cardboard is adhered to the cover, *end papers* are glued over the inside panels in order to give the book a neat appearance. The end papers hide where the cover was joined to the cardboard. When the binding is complete, a dust jacket may be applied.

FIGURE 6.15. A machine glues the book's cover onto pieces of cardboard, and then the covers are attached to the pages at the bindery. *The Puzzle of Books* by Michael Kehoe.

Preparing Art for Printing

FIGURE 7.1. Warren Chappell: *Copellia, the Doll with the Enamel Eyes*. Pen and ink and tempera on blue bristol board. The illustration, *left*, is the final illustration; the illustration, *right*, is the red color separation.

"It should be taken for granted that an illustrator of books must know his craft. He should have not only the knowledge of the means of printing, but a deep tactile sense of its capacities. He must be able to project his expression past the plate and the press and onto the sheet, for it is the printed result that is the end view."

WARREN CHAPPELL,
The Illustrator's Notebook

USING THIS CHAPTER

When you illustrate a book, you prepare pieces of art for printing rather than art that is an end in itself. What satisfies *your* eye may not satisfy the eye of a camera or laser. An illustrator must keep in mind the machinery's limitations in reproducing exact replicas of original art.

The preceding chapter has given you an overview of how the various personnel from the publisher and printer work together to bring book art to its final printed form. In the printing process there are many factors that are out of an artist's control once the original art leaves the artist's hands. This fact makes it crucial for every book illustrator to prepare the final art with the utmost care and complete understanding of the effects of his or her artistic choices.

This chapter will introduce artists who have never prepared art for printing to the basic process of making *mechanicals,* or the final art to be printed. It begins with the simplest mechanical to prepare and moves on to the more complicated. Some of the advantages and disadvantages and the special requirements for using various mediums are discussed. Exact recommendations of brands of paper, pencils, and paints are not included, because each artist develops personal preferences and all brands may not be available in each reader's locale. These descriptions serve as an introduction to the procedures. The best way to learn about preparing art for print is to see your art printed and carefully examine what worked as you expected and what did not. This chapter offers suggestions for inexpensive ways to print artwork so that you gain some experience.

If you have had no previous experience or any classes in preparing art for print, take a class on this topic. Often, area vocational/technical schools offer practical courses on preparing art for printing. Many of these schools also teach printing and may print the work of students in other classes. Several books listed in the Resources section for this chapter offer detailed guidance in preparing art for print and may be used in conjunction with this chapter. As you try some of the exercises in the chapter, ask an experienced graphic artist in your community to look at your work and offer suggestions.

USING LIMITATIONS TO YOUR ADVANTAGE

Look upon whatever limitations are given you in your first book assignment as a positive situation. Do not consider working in black and white to be a handicap. Begin by building strong skills in preparing black and white and limited-color art for print. A first book assignment offers many important choices about sequencing, interpretation, and pacing the illustrations. Each illustration will require much thought and labor and is bound to present new problems for you to solve. The addition of preparing color mechanicals adds another dimension that is best put off until the other aspects of illustration are mastered. Color work is so expensive to print that editors must see if a new artist can meet a deadline and execute a well-conceived book before allowing the artist to work in color. Some well-known illustrators choose to work with limitations even when their reputations allow them total freedom in their art. Arnold Lobel states, "Sometimes limitations are an asset. If I don't have limitations I make some myself, such as size and color. Becoming a professional is knowing what is most comfortable for you."[1]

Exploring One-Color Line Art

The term *line art* may be misleading, because it refers to art that is made not just from solid lines but from any areas of equal tonal value. In line art, the artist may use one or several techniques to create the illusion of shading through manipulating the black-and-white spaces. In *Where the Wild Things Are*, Maurice Sendak shows a masterly use of crosshatch. Randolph Caldecott and Ernest Shepard (See Figures 0.1 and 3.3) use sparing lines to create expressive movement. Stephen Gammell (See Figure 2.9) builds up tone through combining many delicate lines. Linda Escher uses a combination of dots and line for her drawing of a stag. (See Figure 7.2.)

The following description of one-color art will use the terms black and white because even if a colored printing ink is chosen, the art is still prepared in black on white paper. Most books are printed using black ink and white paper; however, there can be much variation within this restriction. Straight black ink and bright white paper give a deadened effect to artwork. Reds and yellows may be added to black to enrich it, and off-white shades of paper will create a warmer feeling. The artist should be aware of these choices and suggest possibilities to the editor, who can then discuss the paper and ink requirements with the art director and production manager. Look at the variations of black ink and white paper to see which you think gives particular books a rich

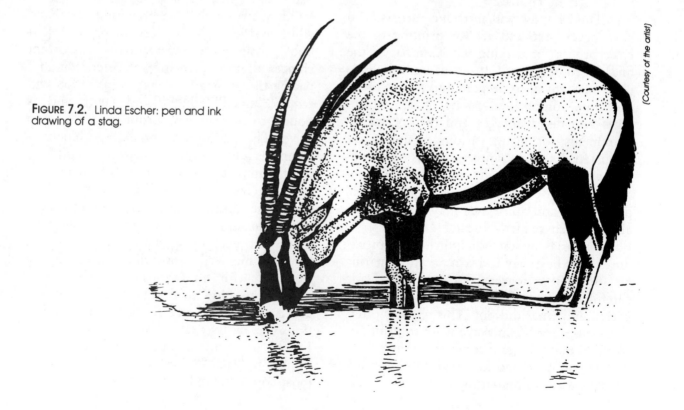

FIGURE 7.2. Linda Escher: pen and ink drawing of a stag.

(Courtesy of the artist)

feeling. Sometimes a color other than black is chosen for printing. *Blueberries for Sal*, a story that Robert McCloskey wrote about a little girl and a bear exchanging places while picking blueberries, was appropriately printed in deep blue.

Before beginning the actual preparation of final art on a book assignment, the artist should know the exact type of paper and the color of the printing ink to be used for printing. The artist must have this knowledge in order to control the effects of the media being used in the final art. This important information should be clarified with the editor so no one has any surprises in the end.

All line art must be executed in a dense black medium. If the artist uses ink, India ink is best. Felt-tip markers do not reproduce well. If pencil is being used, the lead must be soft enough to produce strong lines for the camera. The right paper and illustration board must be chosen. A textured paper or board, for example, may expand the range of simulated tones that an artist may achieve with a pencil.

Exercise 1: Choosing New Art Materials

Before beginning any of the other exercises in this chapter, you may want to spend some time experimenting with new black-and-white mediums. Even though you may have tried different black-and-white materials in the past, now you have the goal of producing art that will reproduce well. If you live in a city with good art supply stores, take time to browse and discuss materials with salespeople. If you live in a area with limited access to art supplies, consult the Resources section, for this chapter lists some major art suppliers who will provide catalogs for mail orders.

Following is a general list of the types of materials to look for that will be useful for the exercises in this chapter.

Paper and Illustration Board: Several types of high-quality drawing paper and board with smooth and textured surfaces. Tracing paper and professional-quality vellum should also be on hand for preparing art for print.

Drawing Tools: Selection of soft pencils and graphite sticks, lithography crayon, brushes for India ink, and drawing pens with a selection of points to be used with India ink.

Inks and Paint: Black India ink, acetate ink (specially treated to cover acctate), black tempera paint.

Acetate: Prepared acetate (may also be called treated acetate) which can be used for overlays and regular India ink, frosted acetate (may also be called matte acetate), and textured acetate. These are less expensive when purchased in rolls, but for experimental purposes, purchase in small quantities.

Exercise 2: Looking at Line Art in Children's Books

Following is a list of illustrators, both contemporary and historical, whose work in line shows the great variation that is possible with limited media. Many examples of books illustrated by these artists are available in libraries.

Edward Ardizonne
Erik Blegvad
Randolph Caldecott
Fritz Eichenberg

Leonard Everett Fisher
A. B. Frost
Robert Lawson
Howard Pyle
Maurice Sendak
Ernest Shepard
Uri Shulevitz

Exercise 3: Experimenting with Black and White Mediums

The books you have studied may have given you some new ideas about the possibilities of illustrating with line. Take some of the new art supplies and experiment with ways to create tones and textures. Try new combinations of paper and pencil or a different pen point. How can you manipulate the areas of black and white to create the effect of tonality? Start by drawing simple objects in your home. If you feel successful with a particular technique, develop a final drawing based on

subject matter from the Chapter 2 drawing exercises. Repeat this procedure with several black and white techniques. This new limitation may help you discover strengths you never imagined.

Size Considerations

The choice of size in preparing the final art can have a great impact on the quality of the printed art. It is important for artists to understand the effects of reduction and enlargement. An artist may feel less restricted when working in a large format and choose to have the final art reduced before printing. If you plan to have work reduced, then it is crucial to know the exact effects of reduction. Delicate pen lines can fade away to nothing. Small dots used for shading can blur into a blotch. Reduction also can take away small mistakes caused by an unsteady hand and improve art by tightening it up. The best way to make your own decisions about what size to work in is to see beforehand what

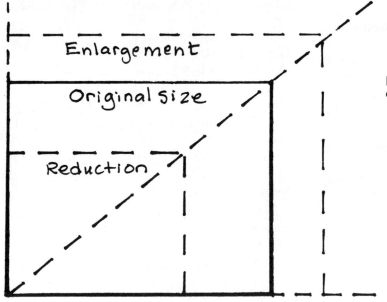

FIGURE 7.3. How to reduce proportionally.

FIGURE 7.4. Test sheet showing how different pencil and pen lines reduce 75 percent.

graphite stick

ebony pencil

8B pencil

6B pencil

4B pencil

HB pencil

5H pencil

6H pencil

#1 litho crayon

#3 litho crayon

brush + ink (6116 isabey)

brush + ink (504 delta)

crowquil pen + ink

513 point + ink

A-5 point + ink

A-4 point + ink

reproduced at 75%

your art looks like reduced in various percentages. If you are reducing your work, remember that the proportions of the final art size must match the page size. Figure 7.3 shows how to reduce proportionately.

Exercise 4: Experimenting with Reduction

Fortunately, modern copying machines offer a quick and inexpensive way for you to see the effect of reduction on your work. Make a simple line drawing using the method you found to be successful in Exercise 3. Also, prepare a sample sheet, testing out different pencil and pen lines and methods of shading similar to Figure 7.4. Take the drawing and sample sheet to a quick-print company with a copy machine that can reduce them various percentages for a minimal cost (25 cents). Make sure that the operator marks the percentage of reduction. Examine the results to see how much reduction your work can sustain without losing quality or how much re-

(Courtesy of the artist)

Deer mouse

FIGURE 7.5. Linda Escher. Pen and ink drawing of a mouse reduced twice.

duction helps to tighten up your work. Figure 7.5 shows how Linda Escher's mouse drawing changes as it is reduced two times.

Requirements for a One-Color Line Art Mechanical

The mechanical must be done directly on illustration board or on paper mounted on a board. A two-inch border is left around the edges of the art. Both paper and board must be kept free of smudges or any marks, because the camera cannot distinguish between wanted and unwanted markings. *Crop marks* indicate the edge of the page for the printer. Protect the art with a tissue-paper overlay.

When artwork extends all the way to the edge of the page, it is called a *bleed*. A mechanical for a page that bleeds has special requirements so that the camera person has a margin of error when photographing the art. The art on a page that bleeds should extend one fourth of an inch beyond the border. This prevents any unwanted white space at the edge of the page. (Crop marks and bleed can be seen in Figure 7.7 on page 108.)

Any special instructions to the printer can be written on the protective tissue paper or with a nonphoto blue pencil on the border. A nonphoto blue pencil is also a good tool for making initial sketches on the mechanical, since its light-blue tone is not recorded on the black-and-white film.

Exercise 5: Making a Mechanical for One-Color Line Art

Use the preceding guidelines to prepare a piece of black and white line art for a printer. You may use one of your drawings from a previous exercise for this purpose. The mechanical will make a good sample for your portfolio because it demonstrates that you know how to prepare a piece of art for the printer.

Requirements for a One-Color Tonal Art Mechanical

The artist uses the same steps to prepare a piece of art with shading. The difference in treatment comes after the art is complete. Tonal art must be screened, or broken up into thousands of tiny dots, before it can be made into a printing plate. This gives tonal art an additional variable that is eliminated in line art. Line art is directly photographed onto the printing plate. The screening required for tonal art can change the original. The artist can minimize any changes by understanding the effect of a camera on tones.

When the camera photographs tonal art, it tends to compress the shades. This makes it necessary to exaggerate contrasts in order to make a tonal variation clear. Shades that are too close to one another can become muddy. A too light background tone can fade right into the white of the paper. There should be at least a ten percent difference between the background tone and the paper. The best way to find out what works well for your own art is the experience of seeing it printed. Talk to other artists who have had extensive experience preparing art for print and ask to see their original and printed art.

Another important consideration in pre-paring the mechanical for one-color tonal art is the amount of reduction. What looks perfect on the original can become a blur if the piece is reduced too much. If you have concerns, you can experiment reducing tonal art, as suggested in Exercise 4.

Some of the materials that are commonly used for one-color tonal art in children's books are pencil and watercolor or India ink washes. Study the work of the following artists before trying your own final art, using one of these mediums:

Tony Chen: *In the Land of Small Dragons* (Ann Nolan Clark)

Michael Deraney: *Yussel's Prayer* (Barbara Cohen)

Anne Dowden: *Wild Green Things in the City*

Charles Mikolaycak: *The Man Who Called Down Owls* (Eve Bunting)

Uri Shulevitz: *The Golem* (Isaac Bashevis Singer)

Ed Young: *The White Wave* (Diane Wolkstein)

Exercise 6: Making a One-Color Tonal Art Mechanical

Follow the same directions for making a mechanical used for Exercise 5. Remember that your art should exaggerate the contrasts in order to reproduce well. Use one of the subjects from the drawing chapter so that your piece of final art will be suitable for your portfolio. Figure 7.6 is a piece of tonal art from Chris Dyrud's portfolio.

If you have not had the experience of seeing your work printed, you could choose a subject that would be an appropriate note card or holiday card. After you have completed the art, take it to a printer for screen-

FIGURE 7.6. Chris Dyrud. Portfolio drawing in pen and ink and ink wash.

ing and printing. This will be an inexpensive way to see your art printed, and the cards will be useful in the future. You can prepare two or four cards and gang them together on the same piece of board. The printer can do the screening and printing together at a cost savings to you, and you also will benefit by seeing the printed results of several pieces of art. Talk to the printer before beginning your project to find out any special requirements that can offer cost savings or a better result.

MULTICOLOR MECHANICALS

The introduction of color to illustration increases the variety and complexity of a book. Color can add to a book's appeal, but if it is not used well, it can detract or distract. It becomes especially important for a book illustrator to understand how colors reproduce in order for the final art to retain the same qualities as the original.

The previous chapter discussed machine methods of separating out color in order to make the films for the printing plates. The next section of this chapter will explain how an artist separates colors for the printer. As

you read about the complexity of this process you may wonder, "Why do I have to spend countless hours doing this when technology can do the same thing much faster?" Publishing practices have come to expect artists to preseparate their own art if only two or three colors are used. This saves the expense of the machine separations. Some artists prefer to do their own separations because they feel they have more control over the results. If you develop a special ability in the art of preseparating, you may be able to achieve effects that are not possible with machine separations.

One artist who is a master of the art of preseparation has written an excellent book on the subject. In *Color in Reproduction*, Hilda Simon states, "Any artist engaged in preseparations has to be aware of all the factors capable of influencing his color effects in the eventual printed image. The greatest challenge, however, is the accurate evaluation of the almost unlimited variety of color combinations and their translation into color percentages."[2] This statement summarizes the special problem posed by manual color separations. Not only does the artist have to prepare a separate mechanical for each color, but the artist has to be able to translate the colors into percentages of gray tones and to envision what the colors will look like in combination. This may sound like an overwhelming task. Although it is not a process that can be learned quickly, new artists can learn to master preseparation techniques if they are willing to experiment with colors, take time to analyze colors, and start with simple and build up to more complex combinations. The exercises that follow in this chapter will introduce you to the process. The book *Color in Reproduction* serves as a detailed guide through this process. Many color charts also are available to help you in evaluating percentages of colors.

Exercise 7: Practice in Analyzing Colors

If you never have thought about the composition of colors in objects that you see around you, beginning to think in this manner is a good first step toward mastery of color separating. Look at the colors in objects around you and make notes about what you see. Look at children's books printed in two or three colors and note what combinations you think the artist used to obtain a new shade. Read about color theory if you never have studied it. Several books in the Resources section for this chapter provide good explanations of color theory. Check to see if a class on color theory is available in your community.

Making Two-Color Mechanicals

Any two colors in combination is called two-color art. Usually one of the colors is black and the second color is any nonprocess color.

The reason for using a nonprocess color for the second color is that a mixed color will offer the widest variety of hues when combined with black. Bright colors when mixed with black produce the strongest results. The second color must be used in different percentages of the same color. For example, you should not combine a red-orange with a red-purple in the same illustration. Many rich colors can be made by combining black and another color, and you may make colors that cannot be made any other way. The green achieved by mixing black and yellow can be just the brightness of a newly sprouted leaf in springtime. When more black is added, the dark hue makes it exactly the color of an avocado. These hues of green are different from what you get by mixing blue and yellow.

The choice of the second color should be dictated by the subject matter. A book with many nature subjects lends itself to green or brown. In *Dandelion*, Don Freeman chose a deep yellow tone for the second color, which was just right for a book about a lion named Dandelion.

When preparing a mechanical for two-color art, some liberties may be taken that are not possible when more colors are used.[3] Mediums may be effectively mixed, such as watercolor and pencil. Once more colors are added, the camera has difficulty deciphering the layers of mixed media. Two-color art also allows the artist to combine areas of flat and tonal color.

Exercise 8: Experimenting in Black and a Second Color

Try to see how broad a spectrum of colors you can achieve by mixing black with a second color. Repeat this exercise several times, changing the second color. Indicate next to

FIGURE 7.7. Nancy S. Hands: *Kara Meets the Macabbees*. Pencil drawings showing crop marks, bleeds, and registration marks.

FIGURE 7.8. Nancy S. Hands. Overlay for Figure 7.7. Ink wash.

the test swatches what percentage of black and the second color you have used to produce a new color. Save these test sheets for reference when doing preseparations.

Several books in the Resources section have color charts that can help you figure out exact percentages of colors. Use the charts to help you with the experimentation. Once you are comfortable with the range of new colors you can achieve with two colors, you are ready to make a mechanical for two-color art. Some books that you may wish to study for the use of two-color preseparated art are:

> Cindy Szekers: *Night Noises* (Tony Johnston), using red and black
>
> Brinton Turkle: *Deep in the Forest*, using gold and black
>
> Hilda Simon: *Wonders of the Butterfly World*, using orange and black, blue and black, yellow and black, and green and black.

Exercise 9: Preparing a Two-Color Tonal Mechanical Using the Overlay Method

The first step in preparing a two-color mechanical is to make a key drawing on illustration board. The key drawing is made for the most complicated color, which is usually black. The drawing must be done in a dense black medium. After the key drawing is complete, registration marks must be affixed in at least three places outside the border of the art. (See Figure 7.7.) The registration marks are crucial to make sure that the second color falls in proper alignment with the first. Printed registration marks may be purchased in quantity at an art supply store.

An overlay may be made using one of several methods, depending on the medium you are using and your own personal prefer-

ence for working. Acetate is a clear plastic that comes with either a prepared surface that accepts regular India ink and paint, or an untreated surface that must be used with specially treated ink. Some acetate is textured, which is good if you are using pencil or inks. (It may be called matte or frosted acetate.) When precise detailed art requires exact registration, acetate may not provide the most stability. Vellum, a special translucent paper, is another choice for an overlay. It can be made completely transparent by working over a light box. Some artists use drawing paper overlays with a light box. Tracing paper may be used as an overlay for pencil art.

The overlay should be taped on top of the key drawing, with registration marks in exact alignment with the key drawing. (See also Figure 7.8.) There are several ways a second color can be employed, from simple application to a more complicated blend. Begin with a decorative use of a second color by applying it sparingly as a flat tone. As you begin to feel comfortable with the process you can try a more complicated mix of colors. If you were actually illustrating a book, the text would suggest whether a complex mix of washes is appropriate or if flat-spot application of a second color is better. In making the overlay, it is important to overlap the area of color slightly into the line or shape on the key drawing. This is important in case there is any shrinkage of paper or slight misregistration upon printing. It ensures no lapses of white space where color should be.

If this exercise were an actual book assignment, before any final art was begun you would make sure that you knew exactly what color ink was to be used by the printer and what type of paper the art was to be printed on. Any change in inks would change the results of your work, and papers can also change the color effects. For the purpose of this exercise, choose a color to work with that matches the printer's colors. The Letraset system is a tool that shows colors that match printer's inks and breaks down colors by percentages. The swatch book is printed on a transparency, which allows you to experiment with different combinations to see what new colors you can make.

Sample swatch books are available from printers. When you prepare your overlay, you should always glue a swatch of the color for the printer so he can match it to the correct printing ink.

The actual work of translating color combinations into shades of gray takes practice. If you train your eye to see in this way, it will become easier for you. The color charts help greatly in this process.

Exercise 10: Preparing a Two-Color Mechanical with the Color-Break Method

A second method of preparing a two-color mechanical is called the color break. This method is useful when there is not a complicated use of the second color and the second color occurs on isolated areas of the page. A nonfiction book illustrated in two colors may take advantage of this method, or a book with spots of flat color. Directions are given to the printer on a vellum or tissue-paper overlay, indicating where the color will go.

The first step is to make the key drawing on illustration board. Next, registration marks are placed on at least three borders. The overlay is taped at the top and registration marks are aligned with the key drawing. The artist outlines the areas to be printed in the second color using red ink. The red lines serve as boundaries for the printer to indicate where the second color will go. The red lines do not print. Within each area, the artist must indicate the percentage of the second color to be printed. A swatch of the second color of the printer's ink to be used must be attached to the overlay. (See Figure 7.9 for a color-break mechanical.)

Prepare your own mechanical using this method. Several of the books listed in the Re-

FIGURE 7.9. Mechanical for a two-color illustration using the color-break method.

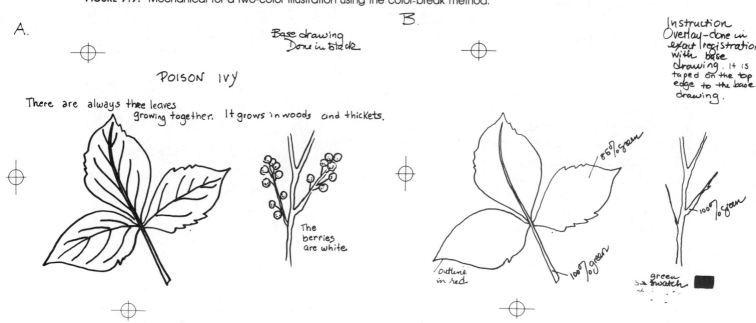

sources section contain visual examples and detailed directions of this method of making a mechanical.

Exercise 11: Printing a Sample of a Color Separation

If you have never prepared a color separation for print, you can design cards or note paper that will serve the purpose of being useful as well as the chance to see how well your color separations work. A possible source for inexpensive printing is your local vocational/technical school, where students may print your work for cost of materials only. Another way to save money on color printing is to work with a friend and choose the same second color for printing. The color plates can then be grouped together (known as "ganged" in printing terminology) and you can split the cost. If you wish to print color work yourself, talk to several printers and enlist their advice and compare prices. Also, ask to look at samples of their printing so that you know if they will do a good job of printing your art. Both your sample color separation and printed piece will make excellent material for your portfolio.

Preparing a Mechanical for Three or More Colors

The basic process of preparing a mechanical for three, four, or more colors is the same as described for two colors. Each color adds another layer to the mechanical and much more variety of color combinations. It becomes even more important for the artist to understand the composition of colors and the effects of colors upon one another in order to produce the best possible work. The decision as to the exact method to use will depend on the nature of the medium, the book's budget, and the customary procedure at a particular publishing house.

The way you choose to prepare your art will depend on its complexity. For multicolor mechanicals, an editor may be able to provide ways to cut down on your time by enlisting the help of the printer. One such method is to have the printer make blue-line prints of the key drawing for each color on a page. (The illustration for Figure 7.1 by Warren Chappell was prepared this way.) The artist provides the key drawing and the printer provides blue-line prints on illustration board, one for each color. The artist fills in gray percentages in the correct area for each color and indicates which board is which color with a swatch. The blue lines do not photograph, and the artist is saved the work of redrawing. This method works best when hairline, or very exacting, registration is not required, because printing plates can shrink slightly from the size of the blue proof copies.

Donald Carrick has developed his own method of three-color separations, as was described in chapter 3. The mechanicals for his work are included in this chapter so you may closely examine one artist's way of working. Figure 7.10 is the green plate. He uses dark green rather than black for his base color. This gives his work soft edges and makes some unusual color combinations. Figure 7.11 is the yellow plate and Figure 7.12 is the red plate. The paintings were done with ink washes and pencil on drawing paper over a light box. He is able to maintain the feeling of spontaneity in his paintings with the three repetitions. Plate 2 is a watercolor study for the final page for which the separations were made. Plate 3 is the final art from page twenty-seven of the book. A

FIGURE 7.10. Donald Carrick: *Lost in the Storm* (Carol Carrick). This separation will be photographed in order to make the dark green printing plate.

FIGURE 7.11. Donald Carrick: *Lost in the Storm* (Carol Carrick). Color separation in black wash. This separation will be photographed in order to make the yellow printing plate.

FIGURE 7.12. Donald Carrick: *Lost in the Storm* (Carol Carrick). This separation will be photographed in order to make the red printing plate. The combination of these colors can be seen in Plate 3, which shows the final art.

study of Don Carrick's books will be helpful if you wish to develop expertise in three-color separations. Arnold Lobel's illustrations in three colors for several Easy Reader series also make excellent study.

FULL-COLOR MECHANICALS

Complex use of acrylics, oils, watercolors, tempera, chalks, casein, colored pencils, and collage may mean that an illustration cannot be preseparated. The budget for a book may call for machine separation, even if it is possible to do hand separations. Once artists have reached a certain stature within the field, they can make their own choices as to whether they wish to do preseparations or not.

A camera or laser cannot automatically pick up to perfection whatever an artist chooses to draw or paint. It is important to know what will make full-color art reproduce the best, so that illustrations are prepared with that in mind.

Cameras compress color and see certain colors better than others. The compression factor means that contrasts should be somewhat exaggerated and the background must be at least 10 percent of a color so that it won't fade into the paper. Light blue is not seen well and should be heightened in order to reproduce well. Delicate mediums, such as colored pencils, need very sharp delineation in order to avoid muddy results. If a strong black outline is important to the art, then the black must be prepared on an overlay so that it will print well. The art is always either prepared on or fastened to an illustration board with two-inch borders.

Separations to be made by lasers require the art to be prepared on flexible board that will be wrapped around the scanning drum. Scanner drums come in various sizes, and the size of your final art is determined by the most economical arrangement of art on the drum. Usually art is prepared the same size as the printed page, so that as many pieces as possible will fit onto the drum at the same time. The weight of the board is crucial to good results. If the board is too heavy, it cannot be easily wrapped around the drum. If the paper is too light, it may not be stable. Heavily textured watercolor paper can also cause some problems. Fluorescent colors do not work well for laser scanning. Discuss exact specifications with your editor or art director before choosing a working surface and any unusual medium. Often the art director will ask a laser separation company to provide a sample separation to see how well it can be separated.

Requirements of Binding

Before you begin any final art, always make sure that you have discussed how the book is to be bound. In the previous chapter, several types of bindings were described. The type of binding affects how much art may be lost in the gutter, or center, where the book is sewn together. If you are preparing double-page spreads, it is important not to have details of the art fall in the center. One fourth of an inch is lost to the gutter. If an object or person in an illustration crosses the gutter, the artist can compensate by extending the object the extra one quarter of an inch in order to have the two halves match as exactly as possible.

If you have no previous experience preparing art for print, use this chapter as a beginning. All artists must use their own experiences with printing in order to find the best methods for their art. Even with all the precautions mentioned in this chapter and in other books, things can go wrong in printing. Sometimes what works well one time fails the next. The best way to see to it that your art reproduces well is to ask questions and try to be involved as much as possible in the actual printing of the book. Treat every experience as a learning situation. New technology may demand flexibility on the part of the artist and may offer new freedoms. Still, an artist cannot depend on technology to replace excellent craftsmanship. Artists must discover what works well for them and use this knowledge to their fullest advantage.

The Final Step: Publishing

FIGURE 8.1. Diane Goode: *When I Was Young in the Mountains* (Cynthia Rylant). Colored ink and brush. "When I was young in the mountains, Grandfather came home in the evening covered with black dust of a coal mine."

"The book is a collaborative effort. The author, illustrator, editor, and art director each has a vision, and it serves to expand and enrich the work. There must be a feeling of mutual trust and respect for each other's expertise."

DIANE GOODE,
Illustrators of Children's Books, 1966–1976

USING THIS CHAPTER

If you seriously are interested in becoming a published illustrator, the activities in this book have provided material that can be developed into artwork for your portfolio. This chapter suggests what to put in your portfolio and how to present it to a publisher. Information on how to submit manuscripts for publication is also included. The role of agents, copyright regulations, and the importance of marketing are also discussed. Whether publishing your work is an immediate or a future goal, it is important to know about publishing practices and procedures if you wish to work in the field of children's book illustration.

THE PORTFOLIO

The preparation of a professional portfolio is the single most important task confronting you if you wish to become a published illustrator. Your portfolio is the only tool an editor can use to judge whether your artwork is suitable for illustration assignments. Every piece in your portfolio should specifically address the visual problems posed in illustrating children's books. There is no room for student drawings of nudes or abstract oil paintings of landscapes. Such examples may indicate your excellence as an artist, but they do not demonstrate your ability to illustrate a children's book. Every item in your portfolio should be carefully selected for its professional appearance and content appropriate to children's books. The impact of the pieces in your portfolio should show that your drawing has vitality, that you can communicate to children, and that you understand printing. It should also highlight your own particular artistic strengths.

What to Include

Every editor or art director has preferences when it comes to choosing artists. Certain commonalities do exist because all editors look for well-drawn, lively art that demonstrates an ability to reach children. The following guidelines for your portfolio are general enough so that you can tailor the specific pieces to reflect your strengths as an artist. For example, if you specialize in black-and-white pen or pencil work, then there is no reason to include any color work in your first portfolio. If, however, you specialize in watercolor painting or colored pencil, then you could put a limited selection of full-color pieces into your portfolio to highlight your skills. The emphasis should be on limited color and black-and-white for a first portfolio, because these are the types of assignments an editor is more likely to give a newcomer to the field.

Judge each piece that you are considering for your portfolio by asking these important questions:

1. Is this piece of art professional in quality?
2. Is the subject matter suitable for a children's book?
3. Does this piece address a particular problem posed by children's book illustration (for example, characterization or pacing)?

The number of pieces to include in your portfolio should take into consideration that editorial staffs are very busy. They are sure to appreciate a few well-chosen examples as opposed to a large quantity. A dozen excellent examples should convey your ability to illustrate. If you have any doubts about the quality or appropriateness of an example, leave it out.

The Dummy

Including a dummy in your portfolio shows that you can pace a book, draw in sequence, maintain a character, and visualize an entire book. The dummy may be small in size and drawn with preliminary pencil sketches. The drawings should be well enough conceived to show your vision for the book but should not be of final quality.

Use your dummy as a sample to demonstrate your skills. If the person who is reviewing your portfolio recognizes the book possibilities of your dummy, then this will be a wonderful opportunity for you. But if you expect this to happen when you first enter the field, you could be disappointed. The picture book field is very competitive, and you will be more likely to have the opportunity to illustrate a picture book after you have gained experience in the field.

The kind of black and white samples in your portfolio should highlight the mediums that you use best. Include examples of both line and halftone art. If you have an area of special expertise, such as nature drawing, emphasize that. If you limit your subject matter, make sure that you carefully research which publishers will be most interested in your specialty. A first portfolio should have very strong black and white examples.

Color Art

It is important to be able to demonstrate your ability to work with limited color. Include at least one piece in your portfolio that uses black plus another color. If you have developed skill at three-color work, also include one or several samples.

If you excel in a full-color technique, include several. Do not be tempted to have in your first portfolio all full-color art. As mentioned earlier, the high cost of color printing makes a beginning artist an unlikely candidate for full-color assignments. Once you gain experience in the field, you can add more color pieces to your portfolio.

Sample Color Separation

A color separation shows an editor that you understand printing problems and are familiar with a technique that is often asked of new illustrators. Your ability to color-separate may make you the preferred choice for an assignment because the editor does not have to worry whether you will be able to handle it. Choose one of the pieces you used for your limited-color sample and prepare a color separation for it.

Optional Suggestions

Sketches of Children and Animals: Some editors like to look through artist's sketchbooks to see how an artist captures lively action. You may prefer to mat some representative sketches for your portfolio. This saves an editor time in leafing through sketchbooks and gives you the chance to be selective about what you show.

Jacket Designs: Some artists break into book publishing through specializing in book jacket illustrations. Books for young adults and older children may have only an illustration on the cover. If you have the training and ability to design and illustrate book jackets, this may be a good option for you. Illustrating book jackets gives you the chance to prepare your art for print and see the results. It is also a good source for full-color illustration assignments.

PLATE 1 Gail Haley: *Jack Jouett's Ride.* Linoleum cut and watercolor title page.

PLATE 2 Donald Carrick: Watercolor study for page 27 of *Lost in the Storm* (Carol Carrick).

PLATE 3 Donald Carrick. Final illustration for page 27 of *Lost in the Storm.* Printed in dark green, yellow, and red. "When Christopher tried to grab him he pulled away, tearing around Chris in giddy circles, kicking up sand with his hind legs."

PLATE 4 Charles Mikolaycak: *Peter and the Wolf* (Sergei Prokofiev). Colored pencil. "Peter walked in front."

PLATE 5 Barbara Cooney: *Miss Rumphius.* Acrylic with colored pencil painted on gesso-coated percale. "Sometimes she went to the conservatory in the middle of the park."

PLATE 6 Ezra Jack Keats: *The Snowy Day.* Collage. "One morning Peter woke up and looked out the window."

PLATE 7 Margot Zemach: Study for *Mazel and Schlimazel* (Isaac Bashevis Singer). Brush and ink colored inks. "Her yellow eyes seem to say: 'What have I permitted! Have I forgotten that I am queen of all the beasts?'"

PLATE 8 Maurice Sendak: *Where the Wild Things Are*. Pen and ink and tempera. "And into the night of his very own room."

PLATE 9 Uri Shulevitz: *The Treasure*. Pen and ink and watercolor. "He walked through forests."

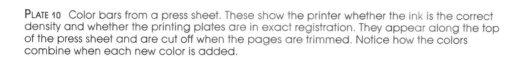

PLATE 10 Color bars from a press sheet. These show the printer whether the ink is the correct density and whether the printing plates are in exact registration. They appear along the top of the press sheet and are cut off when the pages are trimmed. Notice how the colors combine when each new color is added.

yellow plate   magenta plate   cyan plate   black plate

yellow + magenta
plate

yellow + magenta +
cyan plate

yellow + magenta +
cyan + black plate
(full color)

PLATE 11 Charles Mikolaycak: *Peter and the Wolf* (Sergei Prokofiev). Diagram of process colors.

If you have designed a jacket for your sample dummy, then you may choose to include this in your portfolio to show that you have thought about the total conception of the book.

Reproductions of Previously Printed Work: Including artwork that has been printed expands the editor's knowledge of your ability to prepare art for printing. (These samples may break the rule about including only pieces that are the subject matter of children's books.) If you have been working as a graphic artist, you may have many samples to draw from. Try to choose the pieces that come closest to the techniques and content of children's books.

Résumé: A short résumé or brief biographical sketch is important to include if it demonstrates that your previous education and work experience have prepared you for a career in illustrating children's books. Your past experiences may indicate that you have a unique perspective to contribute through your artwork. Do not rely on an impressive résumé to land you an illustrating assignment, however, if your artwork is not excellent.

How to Present Your Portfolio

The contents of your portfolio should be presented in a standard format so that it can be easily looked at. All pieces should be neatly matted and protected with either acetate or a tissue flap. Every piece should have your name, address, and phone number on the back. Attaching a business card to the back of each sample is a professional way to identify your work.

As you prepare your portfolio, make extra copies of several pieces so that you can leave them for a publisher's file, if requested. Samples are important reminders of your work to an editor or art director. The kind of reproductions that you prepare will depend on your budget and the nature of your work.

For line art, high-quality photocopying machines produce inexpensive excellent results. Search your community for a late-model machine that can adjust light and dark. If you find one at a quick-printing service, ask to see a sample of the reproductions from the machine. Black-and-white tonal art does not photocopy well, but you may be able to make an adequate reproduction that will call to mind your work if an editor has seen the original. Color art poses a problem. Slides are the least expensive solution, but some publishers do not like to look at slides and do not wish them left. Color photostats are one option, but they are very expensive. Color-copying machines may make acceptable reproductions, depending on the type of color art you do. Wait to make color copies until after your visit with a publisher. If the person you meet with wishes to have a copy of a piece of color art, ask what form is acceptable, make a note, and send the copy after you return home. This procedure will limit unnecessary expenses.

Where to Take Your Portfolio

If you seriously wish to enter the field of children's book illustration, you must arrange for an interview when you present your portfolio. This will take time and planning, but it can be an educational and rewarding experience.

Every company has its own policies, and you should know as much as possible about a publisher before planning a visit. Chapter 1 suggests that you make note cards to record the books you liked best, with a notation of the publisher on the cards. Return to these cards and find the publishers who produce books that you like. If you did not complete that activity, make a trip to the library or bookstore. Once you have identified several publishers, write and ask them for their juvenile book catalogs. Write the art director to request written guidelines for artists and if (and when) he or she looks at artists' portfolios.

Some companies may review portfolios only once a month. Others may want you to leave your portfolio for one or two days. Find out as much information as you can about what each company requires and take the requirements into consideration when you plan your portfolio presentation. Whenever you write to a publisher, always include a self-addressed stamped envelope. Publishers' high volume of mail makes the SASE a necessity in order to ensure a response. Information about the names, addresses, and type of material published by major publishers is found in an invaluable tool, *Literary Market Place*. This book is located in the reference section of your public library. Another book with similar information is *Writer's Market*. Each book is updated annually.

Start by showing your portfolio to local publishers. Phone contact will make it easy for you to make an appointment. Perhaps you live in a community with no major publishing houses. Check the yellow pages to see if there is a small press or educational publisher within driving distance. Your library may have a book entitled *The International Directory of Small Presses* in its reference section, which lists small presses and their addresses. If you are unfamiliar with what they publish, ask them to send you a catalog

or drive to the company and look at some sample books. The smaller presses and educational publishers are a good source of potential work for a new illustrator. Your earnings may not be as great as with a larger publisher, but there may be less competition as you work to become established in the field.

Whenever you contact a publisher, address the person you write by name. *Literary Market Place* lists names of editors and art directors and makes annual updates. This will assure that your correspondence reaches the right person. In larger publishing houses the art director is in charge of reviewing portfolios. When editors need an artist for a book, they will ask the art director for recommendations. In some publishing houses an editor may look at portfolios. At no time should you send unsolicited artwork through the mail. Publishers cannot assume responsibility for it. If an editor or art director requests to see sample artwork and you need to mail it, either mail copies or, if that is not possible, insure the work and make sure that the recipient knows it is on the way. If you wish to have the artwork returned, include sufficient postage.

For initial contacts with publishing companies, a carefully planned trip to a publishing center may be necessary. Once you have made your first contacts, it will be important to build on positive responses and make return visits as you gain experience in the field and expand your portfolio.

HOW AN EDITOR CHOOSES AN ARTIST

The following description is a general procedure that may vary from company to company and editor to editor, but it gives you a picture of the process of choosing an artist.

When editors of a children's book department have a manuscript ready to be illustrated, they may have in mind an artist whom they think would be perfect for that book. The editor sends the manuscript to the artist and asks if the artist is interested and would supply some sample sketches. If that artist cannot fit the book into a busy schedule or the editor decides to use a new artist, then the editor turns to the art director for help in selecting an artist. The editor and art director discuss the artistic requirements of the book together. The art director looks through the portfolio files for samples of art that would be appropriate to the manuscript. The art director may also look at books published by other companies in search of the right artist. The possibilities are narrowed down to several artists, and the art director shows the editor sample work of the suggested artists. Next, the editor chooses two or three artists and sends them the manuscript, asking for sample sketches to be sent by a specific date. Once the sketches are on hand, editors look for the art they think will best suit the text.

Some other considerations are made by editors when they choose to work with a new artist. The editor must feel confident that the artist can maintain a good working relationship. This is especially important when an editor chooses an inexperienced artist, because the new artist probably will require additional editorial time in preparing the art. A new artist can make an editor feel confident if all conversations and correspondence are handled in a professional manner. The artist should verify every detail of the book's production before beginning the assignment and should feel confident of being able to meet the deadline before accepting the assignment.

After editors look at preliminary sketches, they may want to see a rough dummy and a sample of the final art before offering the artist a contract. Established illustrators often receive contracts without this step because the editor is familiar with the artist's style and way of working.

THE BOOK CONTRACT

The book contract establishes the rights of both the artist and the publisher. It includes the royalty terms, advance on royalties, copyright and subsidiary sales information, amount of artwork expected, and the due date for completion of the art. Before signing a contract, be sure that you can make your deadline. Production schedules for books are very important; books are planned for a fall or spring list for a particular year. If you have any doubts about meeting a deadline, you should discuss with your editor whether you have any flexibility before signing the contract.

When you sign your contract, the publisher will pay you an advance on royalties. This gives you some money while you are working on the art. It is customary for part of the advance to be given at the time of the signing of the contract and the rest upon completion of the art. The advance is deducted from your portion of the royalties once the book goes on sale. This means that it may be a long time before you receive any more money for your work. Books can take a year of production time, and royalties are only sent out one or two times a year. You will not earn any additional money for your work until enough copies of the book have been sold to exceed the amount of your advance.

The illustrator and writer divide the royalties. The standard royalty is 10 percent of the book's list price. If the book is a picture book, then the illustrator receives 5 percent and the author 5 percent. If you illustrate a novel or a book where there is a much greater proportion of writing to art, then the artist receives a flat fee per illustration or a smaller royalty. A beginning artist is usually offered a flat fee for a small number of illustrations for a book. If you can negotiate a royalty rather than a flat fee per piece of art, you usually will earn more money in the long run. Small presses work within tight financial margins and may offer only flat fees for art.

EXECUTING THE ARTWORK

The following description is a generalized version of a typical procedure that may vary from company to company. It shows how the artist and staff of a publishing company work together to produce a book.

Once a contract has been signed by the publisher and the artist, the editor sends the artist specifications for the book. These include the size of the final pages, the number of illustrations, and the color requirements. Artists should verify whether they can make the artwork larger or must work in the same size as the final page. A beginning illustrator is likely to get a previously typeset dummy copy of the book that indicates exactly where the illustrations will fit into the book. An established illustrator is given more freedom in deciding how to divide up the text and where illustrations will be placed.

A pencil dummy is made. The illustrations should be in a form that indicates the plan for the pages but they do not have to be highly polished. (See Figure 8.2 from Julie Downing's dummy page for *Clues in the Desert*, illustrated in final form in Figure 8.3.) One final illustration is completed at this point so that the color scheme can be worked out for printing.

Next, the editor edits the dummy and suggests any changes necessary. Figure 8.4 shows two pages of Priscilla Kiedrowski's dummy for *The Old Fasnacht*, with her editor's initial comments. The art director takes the sample page to the printer to discuss any possible production problems and to make any special arrangements that might be necessary for the printing. Usually the artist is asked to complete the cover art first, because the cover may be used in an upcoming catalog. The cover art can also be used to make color separation proofs.

The artist continues working on the final art and completes the assignment by the date indicated in the contract. The art is turned in to the editor, who makes sure that no changes need to be made. If any changes are necessary, the artist makes them.

The editor and art director now work closely with the production manager to supervise the printing. In some companies, the art director and production manager may be the same person. The production manager or art director checks the films, color separations, and dummy books for any potential problems. Color proofs are checked closely and are shown to the editor and artist. You may want to be involved with the printing process as much as possible so that you can learn from the experience and offer suggestions. Whether this will be possible will depend on your proximity to the printer and the publisher's policies.

FIGURE 8.2. Julie Downing: *Clues in the Desert* (Emmet Davis). Preliminary sketch.

FIGURE 8.3. Julie Downing: *Clues in the Desert* (Emmet Davis). "We walked gingerly down dusty streets and over brick drains that had been built more than five thousand years before."

FIGURE 8.4. Priscilla Kiedrowski: *The Old Fasnacht* (Barbara Mitchell).

HOW MANUSCRIPTS ARE CHOSEN FOR PUBLICATION

It is important for an illustrator to understand how an editor chooses a manuscript to publish. If you wish to both write and illustrate, it is essential to know how to submit a manuscript and what the decision-making process is like. If you do not plan to write, it still is important for you to develop your own criteria for evaluating manuscripts. Illustrating a children's book is a time-consuming process that requires commitment from an artist. If you know what editors look for in manuscripts, it will help you to evaluate manuscripts that are sent to you. You should be willing to pass up an assignment that doesn't feel worthy of your best effort.

Several excellent books have been written by children's book editors that discuss how that editor chooses a manuscript. In *From Childhood to Childhood*, editor Jean Karl discusses how she evaluates manuscripts. She looks for manuscripts that are honest, universal, sensible, enthusiastic, interesting, readable, natural, unified, and positive.[1] These same characteristics can apply to the art in children's books as well. Picture book manuscripts also require the artist to expand upon the text.

Jean Karl describes the specific order in which she considers manuscripts. She begins by looking at manuscripts by authors she already has published. (Often an author signs a contract that gives the publisher first option to publish the author's next book.) She is most interested in authors who have previously published elsewhere, because she assumes that a published writer has already attracted an audience. She then will consider manuscripts that are of special interest to her. Next come manuscripts that are highly recommended by another reader—someone who works in another part of the publishing company, or an agent. Finally, the unsolicited manuscripts are considered.[2]

Other editors may proceed in a different fashion. Established writers are certainly preferred. However, editors may be publishing a series and will be looking for manuscripts that could fit into the series. An unsolicited work by a new author may be just right for the series. Editors may also assign a writer a manuscript on a particular topic. The *Writer's Market* lists the type of material particular publishers are looking for throughout the year. This can be helpful to check for both writing and art submissions. The monthly magazines *The Writer* and *Writer's Digest* also list current needs of publishers. The Society of Children's Book Writers newsletter also contains current publishing information. Some companies will not read manuscripts that have not been requested or solicited. Others actively seek out new authors. Editors feel pride in discovering new talents for both writing and illustrating. Because editorial staffs are often pressed for time and receive a high number of submissions, they must tread a fine line between being open to new writers yet not spreading themselves too thin.

THE DECISION TO PUBLISH

There used to be a time when editors could rely only on their own personal tastes as to what to publish. Economic restraints and reorganization of the structure of many companies has changed this situation. Once an editor has a favorable opinion about publishing a manuscript, marketing factors must be considered before a go-ahead is given.

An editor must first consider what other books have been published on the subject, and how many are still in print. Some of the questions that must be answered are: Is this book unique in some way? Does it offer new information on a subject? How does this manuscript relate to other books planned for upcoming lists? (A wonderful manuscript may not be publishable by a company if they already have planned one or two books on the same or a similar topic.)

Once editors have answered these questions, they must meet with members of the production and marketing departments in order to determine the cost of producing the book and its marketability. Production costs are weighed against sales potential. The sales for the first five years are projected. Children's books tend to sell slowly at first, but good books sell over the course of many years. If the estimates indicate that the book will be profitable to publish, then the editor can offer the author a contract.

MARKETING A CHILDREN'S BOOK

The success of a book is not complete until it begins to sell well. Different types of books are sold in different ways. Trade books are marketed through bookstores and libraries. The work of selling trade books begins when editors circulate to the sales force sales sheets with information about upcoming books. The sales force covers territories and meets with bookstore owners and book wholesalers in order to promote books. The author or illustrator might have some suggestions for promoting the book and should tell the editor. Anything that can make your book stand out on a sales sheet is helpful, to call attention to potential buyers.

Librarians make decisions on what books to order by reading reviews in the major periodicals that review children's books, such as *Horn Book, School Library Journal, Kirkus Reviews, Booklist,* and *Publishers Weekly.* Publishers select certain titles to feature and send review copies to the journals with the hope that the books will be reviewed. Unfortunately, the large volume of books published and the small amount of space in the journals limit the numbers of books that can be reviewed. Well-done books by new authors and illustrators often do attract attention.

One marketing feature that an editor takes into consideration when choosing a new illustrator is to pair the new artist with a known writer. A new writer similarly may be paired with an established illustrator. This practice helps a book's sales appeal because one of the team is already known.

The author/illustrator of a book can promote the book in many ways once it has reached the bookstores. Local bookstores can sponsor book signings and readings. Workshops can be given at schools and in libraries. Local newspapers can be contacted for book reviews and feature articles on the author/illustrator. These kinds of promotional activities can take place in the locale where the author/illustrator currently lives, or in a home town area if the person resides elsewhere. Every opportunity to make your book visible and appealing will help in promoting sales.

Mass-market books, which were described in chapter 5, are sold in a different manner. The large quantity of the editions makes their low cost and high visibility at many retail outlets their prominent sales feature.

SUBMITTING A MANUSCRIPT FOR PUBLICATION

If you are interested in both writing and illustrating or feel that you have the perfect picture book idea this section will briefly describe the procedures for manuscript submission. There are several excellent books on writing for children listed in the Resources section. If you think you may eventually wish to write and illustrate, these books are a must for your reading list. Several of these books describe publishing practices in great detail and offer many helpful suggestions for manuscript submission.

Picture Book Submissions

If you wish to submit a picture book manuscript that you have written and illustrated, send a copy of the double-space-typed manuscript and a copy of the dummy. In a cover letter, let the editor know that you could send a sample of a finished page if he or she wishes to see one. If you have a friend or a relative who has written a picture book manuscript and asks you to illustrate it in order to submit the manuscript and illustrations to a publisher, do not spend time on such a project. Editors wish to choose their own illustrators. Advise your writer friend to submit just the manuscript, so that the writing will be evaluated on its own.

Multiple Submissions

A multiple submission means that the manuscript is sent to more than one publisher at the same time. At one time this practice was not acceptable, but many companies now allow multiple submissions. If you submit a manuscript to more than one company at a time, you must always inform them in your cover letter. A tactful sentence that states that you are submitting this manuscript to several publishers is adequate. Always check the entries in *Literary Market Place* or *Writer's Market* to see if the publisher you wish to contact accepts multiple submissions before you send a manuscript to several publishers at once. It is to your advantage to send multiple submissions, because it can take two to three months before you receive an answer from a publisher due to the many duties of editorial staffs in addition to reading manuscripts.

Rejection Notices

If you submit a picture book or manuscript for publication, you will soon become familiar with rejection notices. Rejection notices range from a form letter or card to a personal response. The form letters are an understandable timesaving necessity. If you receive a personal reply from an editor stating that the material is publishable but does not fit into that company's list at that time, this should encourage you to keep trying elsewhere. Often good material cannot be used because of the nature of a publisher's list. If you receive a letter that suggests making certain changes and resubmitting the manuscript, try to make those changes and send back the manuscript. This means that an editor has already spent some time thinking about your work and is interested in the manuscript. Rejection notices are common. Do not be discouraged, but keep trying.

Many well-known authors received many rejections before their books were accepted for publication.

Agents

Agents perform certain services for a writer or artist in return for a percentage of the writer's or artist's profits on a contracted work. Agents contact publishers for outlets for art and writing, negotiate contracts, and review royalty slips. One advantage of having an agent is that agents develop many contacts at publishing houses and know the book market well. A good agent should be able to direct a manuscript or artwork to the right publisher more easily than a writer or artist may be able to do without the benefits of contacts and precise knowledge of who needs what. Another advantage, which may be very important to some writers and authors, is that you are spared the trauma of rejection notices and the time it takes to contact and recontact publishers. An agent also may be able to negotiate a better contract than an author or artist himself. In return for these services, the agent's commission is 10 percent of the earnings from each project the agent contracts for the client.

Finding an agent may be as difficult as finding a publisher, especially for a beginner. If you know an artist or writer who has an agent, a personal contact may help. Having an agent does not automatically ensure publication. Editors may give special attention to the work of an agent they respect, but an agent cannot guarantee publication.

Agents who work on behalf of writers are called literary agents. Lists of agents who handle children's books are found in several books in the Resources section. The Society of Author's Representatives, at 101 Park Avenue, New York, New York 10017, will provide a list of its members if you wish to send a stamped, self-addressed envelope. You may also request their brochure, *The Literary Agent*.

Artist's agents handle the work of illustrators and find work for them. A list of artist's agents appears in *Literary Market Place*. Artists contact agents and show them their portfolios. A referral from a friend or colleague can be helpful.

COPYRIGHTS

Copyright regulations protect both authors and illustrators. The most recent copyright legislation protects unpublished as well as published work. If you should ever wish to illustrate or quote from something previously published, always write the publisher to check the work's copyright status. You must always acknowledge the source and usually pay a permission fee if the work is to be published. A free pamphlet that fully explains the new copyright law is available from the Copyright Office, Library of Congress, Washington, D.C. 20559.

If you have a piece of art that you wish to copyright on your own, you may also write them for the appropriate forms. There is a ten-dollar fee for each piece that you wish to copyright.

A book contract specifies the copyright conditions. Usually the contract states that the work is copyrighted in the name of the artist or author. If your contract does not do this, ask the publisher to change it so that it is copyrighted in your name.

IN CONCLUSION

If you are just beginning to consider the field of children's book illustration, this chapter introduces you to what lies ahead. Your first step is to achieve a level of excellence in your art. Do not attempt to publish before you are ready. The field is highly competitive. So allow yourself time to become completely familiar with children's books and to develop confidence in your ability to illustrate. You will then be ready to look for ways to use your own special talents to make a positive contribution.

Becoming Part of a Tradition

FIGURE 9.1. J. J. Grandville: *Bizarries and Fantasies of Grandville.*

"The unbroken thread of pictorial art which links the work of artists everywhere throughout history constitutes tradition."

Bertha Mahoney,
Illustrators of Children's Books: 1744–1945

USING THIS CHAPTER

Only in the most recent history of bookmaking have books been written and illustrated specifically for children. In the United States in the past fifty years, children's books illustration has been recognized as an art form in itself. This chapter presents a brief overview of the developments in children's book illustration. Technological developments are described in relation to their impact on book illustration. The Resources section suggests books for in-depth study of specific illustrators and time periods.

Modern illustrators, whose work you looked at in the activities for the first chapter, are but the most recent artists who have illustrated for children. If you study the enduring qualities of artists before you, you can bring a depth to your own work. The purpose is not to imitate the past, for this would lead to superficial art, but to glean from the past and then to synthesize this knowledge with your own strengths, in order to create something that is uniquely your own.

Previous artists had to be resourceful in making the most out of the printing technology available to them. The interdependence between book illustration and printing is an evolving relationship that continues today. Contemporary illustrators have fewer technological restrictions imposed upon them. This should compel them to search deeper within themselves to produce meaningful art. Some of the techniques being used in contemporary children's books may create exquisite effects, but their high polish makes them feel cold and may render these books inaccessible to children. Limitations can produce strong illustrations when the artist reaches beyond what is easy. The timeless qualities of lively pen lines, superb drafts-manship, and effective communication in black and white are examples of working well within limitations. The emerging illustrator today must master drawing and learn to exploit black-and-white and limited-color techniques to their fullest. The economic realities of today can have the positive benefit of forcing artists to achieve excellence with less.

EARLY HISTORY

Until about three-hundred-and-fifty years ago, most children did not handle books. Early books were handwritten and hand-colored. This made them very precious. Adults used the books to give children moral and religious instruction. Medieval bestiaries (See Figure 9.2) decorated with fabulous animals such as unicorns and dragons are examples of the earliest teaching books.

Moveable type was invented in the mid-fifteenth century. This invention made it possible to print large numbers of books at once, but books were still produced for adults only. One of the first books that may have been designed with children in mind was printer William Caxton's edition of *Aesop's Fables*. The fables were illustrated with simple woodcuts.

The first known picture book designed especially for children was the *Orbis Pictus Sensalium* (1658), by Bishop John Comenius. Bishop Comenius disliked the didactic instruction of his time and wanted to teach children language through pictures. The book's content was natural history, and each scientific word was illustrated by a woodcut. (See Figure 9.3.) This book remained popular in Europe for over a century and was reprinted in the United States in the 1800s. The

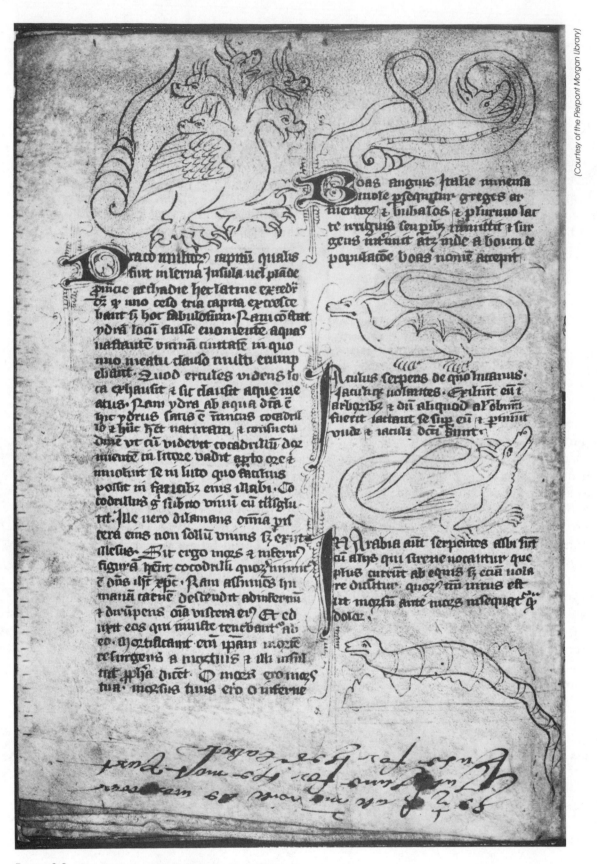

FIGURE 9.2. *The Fountains Abbey Bestiary,* illuminated.

Birds that haunt the Fields and Woods.

FIGURE 9.3. *Orbis Pictus Sensalium,* Bishop John Comenius, 1664.

development of illustrated books continued in the seventeenth and eighteenth centuries with a teaching focus. Books were now designed for constant use by children. Hornbooks were used to teach the alphabet. They contained an alphabet sheet pasted on a piece of wood, with a transparent horn cover. They led to a multi-paged version called a battledore, which taught numbers and reading as well. (See Figure 9.4.) Chapbooks were used frequently to instruct. Small woodcuts illustrated moral lessons.

THE ENGLISH TRADITION

Woodcuts often resulted in poor-quality reproductions because the blocks used for carving deteriorated over numerous printings. Thomas Bewick made a great contribution to book illustration by refining the technique of carving on end blocks of wood. End-grain carving permitted detail not previously possible. Bewick achieved the effects of halftone shading because of the ability of end-grain blocks to accept detail. The resulting images are small and clear, with a great improvement in quality. (See Figure 9.5.) Another advantage of end-grain blocks is that they hold up well after thousands of printings. Bewick also was significant because he was the first artist in modern times to earn a living through illustrating. Many of his illustrations were for children. He was the first in a line of English wood engravers who came

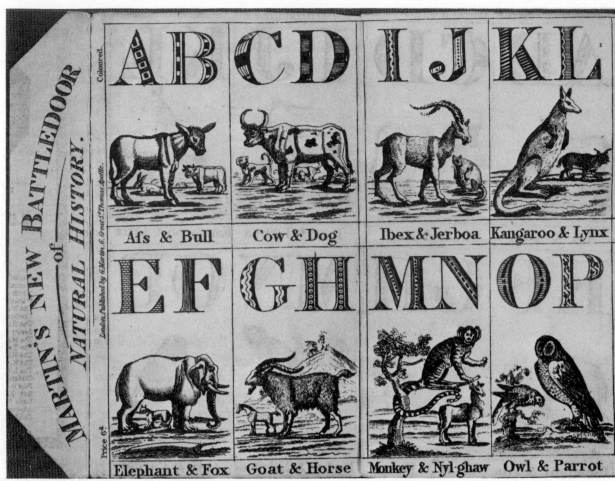

FIGURE 9.4. *Martin's New Battledoor of Natural History,* 1810. Woodcut illustration.

FIGURE 9.5. Thomas Bewick: *Select Fables in Three Parts* (Aesop). Wood Engraving. "The Dog and the Shadow."

FIGURE 9.6. William Blake: *Songs of Innocence.* Copper plate engraving in full color. Cover illustration 1789.

to have a large influence on future book illustration for both adults and children.

In the late eighteenth century, William Blake introduced a different method of illustrating. Using copper etching to make painstakingly hand-printed plates, he produced *Songs of Innocence.* (See Figure 9.6.) Blake was motivated by his own belief in the innocence of childhood. His artwork for this volume unites text and illustration in a way that has characterized good books since his time. Blake was also significant because he began the tradition of great artists illustrating children's books.

John Newbery was a pioneer in publishing attractive books for children. In the middle of the eighteenth century he began publishing books for parents to use to instruct their children. Decorative features, such as embellished end pages, made the books appealing. Text and illustration were designed to blend well. The books were inexpensive, printed in a small format, and intended to reach many children. Many of the Newbery books, on natural history subjects, were instructive. Others, such as Figure 9.7, were for a child's entertainment.

By the end of the eighteenth century, many publishers were producing books for children on the arts, sciences, geography, and history, as well as the standard moral tales of the day. There was also a new interest in fairy tales in the 1700s. In Europe, Gustave Doré illustrated a new edition of Perrault, and Hans Christian Andersen and the Grimm brothers emerged as storytellers. Figure 9.8 is a Doré illustration for *Les Contes de Perrault*.

English artist George Cruikshank produced notable illustrations for fairy tales. His work reveals continued improvements in the technique of wood engraving. (See Figure 9.9.) Previously, artists had designed their wood blocks and then sent them to craftsmen for cutting. Often the blocks were designed without an understanding of how they could be successfully cut. This lack of knowledge, combined with printing on low-quality paper, resulted in poor reproductions. Cruikshank's ability to design his wood engravings

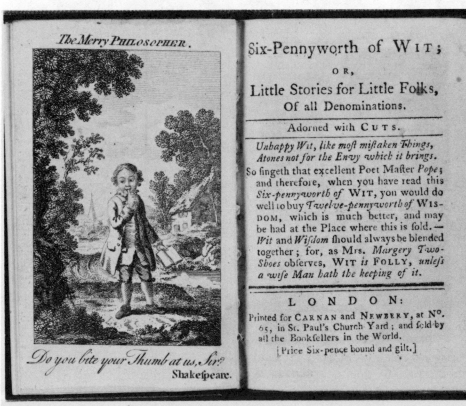

FIGURE 9.7. John Newbery and Sons, publisher: *Six-Pennyworth of Wit: Or, Little Stories for Little Folks, of All Denominations*. (Circa 1769). Woodcut illustration.

(Courtesy of the British Museum)

FIGURE 9.8. Gustave Doré: *Les Contes de Perrault* (Charles Perrault) 1862.

FIGURE 9.9. George Cruikshank: *German Popular Stories* (Grimm) 1823.

with a full understanding of how they would be carved and printed improved the quality of book illustration and set a standard for others to follow. His illustrations were also outstanding because of their vitality and humor.

Edward Lear was another important English artist, because he recognized the importance of fantasy for children. His *Book of Nonsense* has been reprinted recently (See Figure 9.10) to offer contemporary children a taste of his wit and zany imagination. His books were printed by the copper plate etching method. They were printed in large edi-

tions of black and white and then sent out to be hand colored with watercolors, utilizing the cottage industry of families working in their homes. This method for coloring books by hand was common during the first half of the nineteenth century.

The work of printer Edmund Evans brought significant changes to color printing. Evans was the foremost color printer of the 1800s. His goal was to mass-produce profusely illustrated books for children using well-known artists of the day. He believed that children deserved beautiful books and that if he could print enough books inexpen-

There was an Old Man of Coblenz, the length of whose legs was immense;
He went with one prance from Turkey to France,
That surprising Old Man of Coblenz.

FIGURE 9.10. From *A Book of Nonsense* by Edward Lear. Pen and ink and watercolor in full color.

sively, many children would be able to enjoy them. The color illustrations combined the art of wood engraving with the use of oil colors. He used the new invention of photography to take a photograph of the base wood block, which was the color black. Then the photos were transferred to the other blocks, one for each color to be printed. Each block was engraved and inked separately and then printed in registration, one directly on top of the next. Three artists came into prominence working with Edmund Evans: Walter Crane, Randolph Caldecott, and Kate Greenaway.

Walter Crane's illustrations are characterized by flat colors outlined in bold black, which reflect the impact of the Evans's colored printing method. His work emphasized design and decoration (See Figure 9.11) and

FIGURE 9.11. Walter Crane: *Baby's Own Aesop*. Wood engraving in color, title page illustration.

often had decorative borders and embellished end papers and title pages. Many of his illustrations were influenced by Japanese woodcuts. Crane's books were well planned and harmonized text and art. The subjects were frequently rhymes, songs, and fairy tales. Some of his original books have been reprinted and are available in stores and libraries.

Randolph Caldecott's drawings have the appearance of being spontaneous because they are so full of movement. He mastered the "art of leaving out," believing that "the fewer lines, the less error committed."[1] His books are peopled with huntsmen, country characters, and children. Figure 0.1 is a typical Caldecott character. Many of the books were rhymes and songs set in a picture book format. The enduring vitality and humor of his illustrations still capture contemporary audiences.

Kate Greenaway was known for her nostalgic illustrations. Her work became so popular that a whole style of dress was fashioned after the Greenaway girls. She loved to draw English gardens and children. (See Fig-ure 9.12.) Unfortunately, her great popularity led many less-talented artists to imitate her style.

The new color printing methods lent themselves to a style that became popular on the Continent as well as in England. Black outlines, flat color, and emphasis on decorative elements of the book characterized the international style popular at the turn of the century. Each artist working in this style reflected the uniqueness of his country of origin, yet a similarity remained. The work of these artists is available for study through individual volumes produced in recent years and is noted in the Resources section. Some of the artists to look for are Boutet de Monvel of France, Carl Larsson of Sweden, Ivan Biliban of Russia, and Kay Nielsen of Denmark.

Printing advances at the turn of the century permitted better reproductions of watercolors. Full-color illustrations were produced on glossy paper, glued separately into the books. This technological advance promoted the idea of books as beautiful objects, and many books were produced more for the

FIGURE 9.12. Kate Greenaway: *Kate Greenaway's Birthday Book for Children.* Watercolor in full color.

FIGURE 9.13. Leslie Brooke: *Johnny Crow's Garden Party*. Pen and ink. "The camel swallowed the enamel."

adult audience than for the child. Some of the books of Edmund Dulac and Arthur Rackham reflect this trend.

Two artists whose work reflects a special concern for children did rise to prominence during this period: Beatrix Potter and Leslie Brooke. Beatrix Potter's ability to capture the intimate world of the small child has not been surpassed. Her small naturalistic watercolors of country animals and their environments continue to be cherished by today's children. Her books marry art and text, creating a feeling of wholeness. She demonstrated the importance of having an affinity for your subject matter—perhaps the best legacy she could leave to future illustrators. Her love of small animals and their environments began at an early age, and this intimate knowledge of her subjects comes across clearly in her art. (See Figure 1.4.)

Leslie Brooke's work also continues to delight children. His books are filled with animals engaged in humorous antics. *Johnny Crow's Garden Party* (See Figure 9.13) exemplifies Brooke's lively characters and enjoyment of rhymes.

CHILDREN'S BOOKS IN AMERICA

The twentieth century brought the hub of publishing to the United States. An American tradition in children's book publishing grew out of English publishing practices and the influence of new immigrant artists. Contemporary art styles, such as impressionism and expressionism, also had an impact on illustrators. A uniquely American art form began to emerge in America as books were produced in larger numbers due to new power presses and other printing innovations.

In 1893, Anne Carroll Moore established the first children's book room in a public library. The New York Public Library children's book room had excellent books produced in Europe as well as new American books. It became a place to go to look at the best in children's books. As children's librarians, such as Moore, began calling attention to excellence in children's books, publishers responded. This began an alliance between librarians and editors that has had an impact on juvenile publishing ever since. In 1918,

143

Macmillan was the first major publisher to establish a children's book department. Doubleday followed four years later.

The founding of *St. Nicholas Magazine for Boys and Girls* was an important impetus for writers and illustrators at the turn of the century. The goal of the magazine was to inspire children with "an appreciation of fine pictorial art, cultivate imagination, foster love of beauty, stimulate ambitions, and impart high ideals to children."[2] This devotion to quality encouraged many of the best writers and artists of the day to turn their attention to children in *St. Nicholas*. Many now famous books, such as Kipling's *Jungle Books*, had their start in *St. Nicholas*.

Another positive influence on the atmosphere for creating children's books in early twentieth-century America was the Boston Bookshop for Boys and Girls. This bookstore became a mecca for people interested in purchasing quality books for children. *Horn Book* magazine was an outgrowth of the bookstore. Its first issue in 1924 stated, "We blow our horns for the best in Children's Literature, for books beautifully written and finely illustrated. . . ."[3] *Horn Book* continues to champion quality writing and illustrating through its informative articles and book reviews.

The earliest American illustrators of note studied in Europe and drew on the European tradition for their work. E. Boyd Smith worked in the international style but his content was purely American. His pictures included children from the many cultural backgrounds that comprise the American population in the American countryside. A contemporary of Smith began to forge a new American style. Howard Pyle began a school in which he taught a select group of students. Henry Pitz wrote that Pyle's favorite phrase was "Throw your heart into your picture and jump in after it."[4] The spirited characters that people Pyle's illustrations reflect his involvement in his art. His lively portrayals of country scenes brought a new vitality to American illustration. Although his subjects were European, his bold figures drawn with firm, lively pen lines were a departure from the current European style. (See Figure 9.14.)

FIGURE 9.14. Howard Pyle: *Pepper and Salt.* Pen and ink. "Clever Peter and the Two Bottles."

FIGURE 9.15. Ingri and Parin d'Aulaire: *The Terrible Trollbird*. Photograph of a lithographic stone used for the illustration.

By the end of the twenties, the children's book industry was well established in the United States, with many artists now working in the field. More libraries had established children's rooms, and more publishers had begun separate children's departments. Improved printing technology also had its impact. The process of lithography was adapted to offset power presses. The new presses used a better grade of paper and produced finer results. Faster printing permitted larger editions to be run less expensively. Artists began to develop new techniques for preparing art for print. The books began to have new looks with double-page spreads. Advances in typesetting equipment permitted greater freedom in designing book formats.

Several inventive artists came on the scene in the thirties. Wanda Gag used a horizontal format in her still-popular *Millions of Cats*. The illustrations actually break right out of their rectangular border. She, like other American artists during this era, drew on her European folk heritage for subject matter. Her rich black and white illustrations make excellent studies for artists today.

Color predominated in the art of several of the other immigrant artists. Ingri and Parin D'Aulaire adapted stone lithography for preparing art for book printing. They translated colors into shades of gray on zinc plates. The plates could then be printed in the correct color without the intermediary step of photography. This resulted in illustrations that appear to be hand drawn. Figure 9.15 is a photograph of one of the lithographic stones that was used to make *The Terrible Trollbird*.

From Russia came Feodor Rojancovsky, who also worked in full color. His fuzzy animals and chubby children invited children to touch them. His cheerful characters made lively appearances in children's books for three decades and still enjoy popularity. Another Russian countryman, Boris Artzybasheff, was influenced by the art nouveau movement. His illustration from *Aesop's Fables* shows his ability to design black on white or white on black. (See Figure 9.16.)

Another newcomer to America gave children many characters to remember over the years. All of Roger Duvoisin's animals have distinct personalities. His strong and sure pen lines combine with an air of spontaneity, excellent design, and marvelous sense of humor to produce many noteworthy books. Roger Duvoisin's art was as varied as the many texts he illustrated. He was capable of capturing soft moods, as in *Hide and Seek Fog*, as well as the memorable adventures of Petunia or the Happy Lion.

In the thirties, a group of American-born illustrators rose to prominence. Their style showed a concern for precise draftsmanship—whether they worked in pen, pencil, dry brush, or lithography crayon. Their subjects were thoroughly American, and they were equally talented at writing and illustrating, receiving recognition for both. Robert Lawson carried on the tradition of strong black and white pen drawings. His drawing for *The Treasure of the Isle Mist* shows delicacy and detail, and creates a wonderful sense of atmosphere. (See Figure 2.1.) The

ever-popular Ferdinand demonstrates his remarkable ability to characterize both humans and animals. James Daugherty's illustrations were filled with movement and an expressive use of line. *Andy and the Lion* is a classic picture book, while *Daniel Boone* is a fine example of a book for older children.

Robert McCloskey emerged on the scene with *Lentil* in 1940. His characters in *Homer Price* (See Figure 1.5), *Centerburg Tales*, and *Lentil* memorably portray growing up in the Midwest. Later books depict special American places on the East Coast, such as Boston in *Make Way for Ducklings* and Maine in *Time of Wonder*.

In the forties, the importance of creating books for the very young child was recognized. The master storyteller for this age group was Margaret Wise Brown. She was such a prolific writer that many artists had the opportunity to illustrate her books. Clement Hurd illustrated *The RunAway Bunny* and *Good Night Moon*. (See Figure

FIGURE 9.16. Boris Artzybasheff: *Aesop's Fables.* Pen and ink. "The Tortoise and the Hare."

Studies for Runaway Bunny
CH 1941

FIGURE 9.17. Clement Hurd: *The RunAway Bunny* (Margaret Wise Brown).

9.17 for a preparatory sketch for *The Run-Away Bunny*.) Leonard Weisgard won the Caldecott Medal for *The Little Island*, a Margaret Wise Brown book written under the pseudonym Golden MacDonald. Jean Charlot, master lithographer and muralist, illustrated *Two Little Trains*. (See Figure 9.18.) Garth Williams illustrated *Wait Until the Moon Is Full*. Each of these artists illustrated other Brown books too and went on to make significant contributions to children's literature over subsequent years. Their work uses many different styles and mediums and has remained in print. Well-worn copies can be found in libraries in every community.

In the fifties, an expanded book market was caused by the baby boom and the growth of school libraries. Children's book departments grew to meet these needs. Graphic designers began illustrating children's books. This tradition has carried into the present, with artists such as Leo Lionni (See Figure 6.1) and Eric Carle (See Figure 4.2) illustrating children's books. Books were well designed and stepped out of conventional rules. Color was in high demand, and

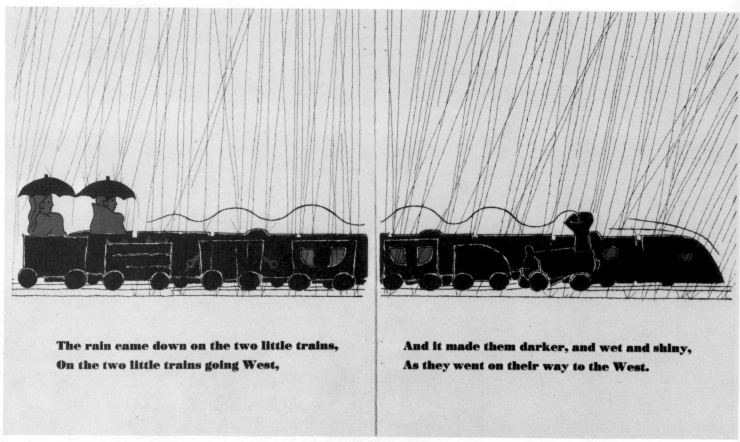

**The rain came down on the two little trains,
On the two little trains going West,**

**And it made them darker, and wet and shiny,
As they went on their way to the West.**

FIGURE 9.18. Jean Charlot: *Two Little Trains* (Margaret Wise Brown). Lithograph.

artists perfected skills in preseparating colors to keep production costs lower. New typesetting techniques encouraged innovations in page design. Improved methods of offset printing gave artists more flexibility in choosing a medium.

Marcia Brown began her career in the fifties and continues to make her presence felt in children's books today. The particular medium or style she uses in a book is always a response to the particular text. A study of her books and the articles about illustration she has written over the years in *Horn Book* are thought-provoking. Figure 3.1 is from her Caldecott award-winning *Once a Mouse*.

The social significance of childhood was recognized in the sixties. This resulted in books that included children of all racial and social backgrounds.[5] Every child was portrayed as being worthwhile. Federal entitlement programs increased the amount of money available to schools and libraries for book purchases. As a result, more money was available to produce books and many previous restraints on production were removed. Books blazed in color and rolled off the presses in increasing numbers. Opportunities opened up for new artists, and different techniques and formats were used.

Ezra Jack Keats is an artist whose subjects and techniques reflected the trends of the sixties. Striking full-color collages and paintings portray the life of an inner-city black child, Peter, in a totally natural manner. *The Snowy Day*, pictured in Plate 6, continues to be a favorite with young children and is an outstanding example of a picture book.

It is appropriate to conclude a discussion of the history of children's book illustration with a look at the work of Maurice Sendak. His work demonstrates the value of studying the past in order to learn from its strengths and then to forge those qualities into something innovative. Within Sendak's work, a kinship with German engravers of the fifteenth century, such as Dürer, can be seen. (Note the texture of the monsters in *Where the Wild Things Are*, Plate 8.) Sendak's lively children in his early work, such as in *A Hole Is to Dig*, are portrayed with simple moving lines that share a kinship with the drawings of Randolph Caldecott (Figure 0.1). *In the Night Kitchen* is influenced by comic books and movies and incorporates the tradition of animating everyday objects that was used by Sir John Tenniel in his famous illustrations for *Alice in Wonderland*. Sendak has also drawn on historic books for creating modern versions of old forms of books. *The Nutshell Library* contains a cautionary tale (*Pierre*), as well as a book of months (*Chicken Soup with Rice*), a book of numbers (*One Was Johnny*), and an alphabet book (*Alligators All Around*).

Although the preceding brief history has been limited to books from western culture, it is important to note the rich eastern tradition in children's book art. Eastern printing technology, for example, is older than western. A Japanese scroll containing frolicking animals illustrated by Toba Soja may be considered the earliest example of a picture book. Velma Varner turned the twelfth-century scroll into a modern picture book called *The Animal Frolic*. (See Figure 9.19.) Today, artists such as Ed Young, Kazue Mizamura, and Tony Chen draw on their wealthy heritage to bring beautiful books to children.

The past leaves us a rich legacy. Weave its enduring qualities into your own art through the use of your imagination.

ACTIVITIES

Visiting Collections of Historic Children's Books and Art

You may be surprised to discover that a library or museum in your vicinity houses original art of historic illustrators. Collectors or the artists themselves may have donated art to a library or museum, making them available for you to study. Some excellent collections to visit are:

Boston, Simmons College Collection
Baltimore, Enoch Pratt Library

FIGURE 9.19. Toba Soja: *The Animal Frolic* (Velma Varner). Brush and ink.

Chadds Ford, Pennsylvania, Brandywine Museum

Chicago, Newberry Library

Minneapolis, Kerlan Collection at the University of Minnesota

New York City, Public Library (main branch) and Pierpont Morgan Library

Philadelphia, Pennsylvania Free Library

Toronto, Osbourne Collection at the Toronto Public Library

If you live near one of these collections or are traveling to the area, you can make a comparison of the original art and its printed version. Some of the collections have examples of the art in its preparatory stages, which is beneficial to study. If you plan to visit one of these or another collection, it is wise to write ahead to find out if there are any special requirements for using the resources.

Looking at Historic Books and Reprints

If original historic art is not available for study in your community, your library may have a rare book collection that contains some of the books or works of artists mentioned in this chapter. Your local library also may have more recent reprints of works by older illustrators for you to study. These books are listed in the Resources section.

Another valuable activity is to study the work of master illustrators from previous time periods to look at what makes their work outstanding. Although these artists did not illustrate for children, their art provides valuable lessons for artists today. Look in your local library for collections of Rembrandt, Goya, Daumier, Doré, Hogarth, Grandville, and Rolandson.

Focus on a time period or an artist you admire and take time to analyze why you are attracted to that artist's work. Try to decide what the artist was trying to communicate in a particular illustration and how this was effectively accomplished. Was it through the use of darks and lights? Was there an emphasis on an unusual perspective? What was the impact of the facial expressions? How was the pictorial composition used to communicate a feeling? What kind of mood was expressed in the illustration? Asking these types of questions about the artwork you study will help reveal the artist's intentions. Learning how others communicated effectively will give you some ideas for your own work.

FIGURE 9.20. Margot Zemach: *Mazel and Schlimazel* (Isaac Bashevis Singer). Brush and ink study for tailpiece.

(Courtesy of the artist and the Kerlan Collection, University of Minnesota Libraries)

Footnotes

CHAPTER 1

1. Selma Lanes, *The Art of Maurice Sendak* (New York: Harry N. Abrams, Inc., 1980), p. 110.

CHAPTER 2

1. James Gurney and Thomas Kincade, *The Artist's Guide to Sketching* (New York: Watson Guptill, 1982), pp. 58–63.
2. Miriam Hoffman and Eva Samuels, *Authors and Illustrators of Children's Books* (New York: R. R. Bowker Company, 1972), p. 315.
3. Hoffman and Samuels, p. 315.
4. Hoffman and Samuels, p. 315.

CHAPTER 3

1. Miriam Hoffman and Eva Samuels, *Authors and Illustrators of Children's Books* (New York: R. R. Bowker Company, 1972), p. 304.
2. Lee Kingman, ed., *Illustrators of Children's Books: 1957–1966* (Boston: Horn Book, 1967), p. 174.
3. Fritz Eichenberg, *Wood and the Graver: The Art of Fritz Eichenberg* (New York: Clarkson N. Potter, 1977), p. 178.
4. Eichenberg, p. 179.

5. Fritz Eichenberg, the 1984 May Hill Arbuthnot Lecture.
6. Eichenberg, *Wood and the Graver: The Art of Fritz Eichenberg*, p. 188.
7. Gail E. Haley, conversation with the author, 1984.
8. Haley, conversation.
9. Gail E. Haley, *Gail E. Haley: Wood and Linoleum Illustration* (Weston Woods: Weston Woods Studio).
10. Leonard Everett Fisher, correspondence with the author, 1984.
11. Fisher, correspondence.
12. Leonard Everett Fisher, *Northlight, The Creed and Craft of Leonard Everett Fisher* (Westport: Fletcher Art Service, July/August, 1973), p. 17.
13. Stephen Gammell, conversation with the author, 1984.
14. Donald Carrick, correspondence with the author, 1984.
15. Carrick, correspondence.
16. Carrick, correspondence.
17. Charles Mikolaycak, correspondence with the author, 1984.
18. Mikolaycak, correspondence.
19. Mikolaycak, correspondence.
20. Mikolaycak, correspondence.
21. Miriam Hoffman and Eva Samuels, *Authors and Illustrators of Children's Books* (New York: R. R. Bowker Company, 1977), p. 237.
22. Hoffman and Samuels, p. 238.
23. Hoffman and Samuels, p. 238.

24. Margot Zemach, correspondence with the author, 1984.
25. Zemach, correspondence.

CHAPTER 4

1. Arnold Lobel, correspondence with the author, 1984.

CHAPTER 5

1. Maurice Sendak, lecture at the New School for Social Research, 1971.
2. Uri Shulevitz, lecture at the New School for Social Research, 1971.

CHAPTER 7

1. Arnold Lobel, correspondence with the author, 1984.
2. Hilda Simon, *Color in Reproduction* (New York: Viking Press, 1980), p. 79.
3. Simon, p. 45.

CHAPTER 8

1. Jean Karl, *From Childhood to Childhood* (New York: John Day Company, 1970), pp. 60–67.
2. Karl, p. 80–87.

CHAPTER 9

1. Bertha Mahoney, *Illustrators of Children's Books: 1744–1945* (Boston: Horn Book, 1947), p. 69.
2. Selma Lanes, *Down the Rabbit Hole* (New York: Atheneum, 1971), p. 22.
3. *Horn Book* (Boston: Horn Book, Volume I, October, 1924), p. 30.
4. Henry Pitz, *Illustrating Children's Books* (New York: Watson Guptill, 1967), p. 70.
5. Barbara Bader, *American Picturebooks From Noah's Ark to the Beast Within* (New York: Macmillan Publishing Company, 1976), p. 368.

Glossary

Bleed: When artwork extends to the edge of the page. The artist must extend art one quarter of an inch beyond the border whenever there is a bleed.

Blueprint or Silverprint: Photographic print made of the whole book after all the elements have been positioned in place. This print is checked by the editor and production manager.

Camera Ready: Art that is ready to be photographed for the films that are made into the printing plates.

Chromalins: Color proofs printed on clear acetate. Each sheet of acetate contains a dust of one of the process colors (magenta, black, cyan, or yellow). The four sheets are laminated into one and are used to check color accuracy and registration.

Color Bars: Used by the printer to check ink density and color on the press sheet. Found along the top edge of the press sheet.

Color Separation: Separating out each color in order to make individual printing plates for each color to be printed. Three types of color separation are discussed in Chapter 7: camera, laser, and hand separation.

Continuous-tone Copy: Image with full range of tones, from light to dark. Also called half-tone.

Double-page Spread: Two pages facing one another in which the illustration extends across both pages.

Dummy: Artist's sample book used to show an editor the conception of the book. A blue-print copy of the book used to check position of all elements of the book also is called a dummy.

End Papers: Sheets at the front and back of the book that attach the pages of the book to its cover. They hide the sewing of the binding. They may be colored or decorated or white.

Flat: Final film of text and illustration taped on plastic sheets ready to be made into printing plates.

Folio: Printing term for a page in a book; the number of a page in a book.

Galley Proofs: Proofs of text printed on long, narrow sheets before being cut into pages; used to check accuracy of text.

Four-color Process Printing: Three colors plus black (lemon yellow, magenta red, and cyan blue), which when combined achieve a full range of color by printing one over the other.

Gutter: Portion of the paper taken up by the binding in the center of the book. Not less than one quarter of an inch, although different bindings have different specifications.

Halftone: Continuous-tone shading, in which gradations are broken into dot patterns in order to make printing plates. Tonality is achieved through the density and size of the dots.

Imposition: Arrangement of the pages of a book on the press sheet in proper sequence, to match the way the book will be folded and cut for binding.

Intaglio: Below-surface printing, in which an etched surface accepts ink and, under pressure, transfers the ink to paper. Artists' form of intaglio: etching, dry point, mezzotint, aquatint, and copper engraving. Commercial form of printing is called gravure and is used to print newspapers.

Key Plate: Base plate in printing that provides the outline for other colors and most of the instructions for the printer; usually black.

Line Art: Solid areas of color of the same tonality. May be dots, lines, or solid shapes. Also called line copy.

Makeready: Preparing the printing press to begin a press run.

Mechanical: Board on which art and text are placed in exact position for the camera. Instructions for the platemaker are included on the border or flap.

Moiré Pattern: Undesirable pattern caused by overlap of dots at incorrect angles.

Offset Lithography: Process of printing in which the image area and nonimage area are on the same plane. Based on the principle that grease and water do not mix. Printed image is offset onto a rubber blanket and then onto paper. Also called planographic printing. Used today for printing most children's books.

Opaquing: Hand process of painting out unwanted areas of color on a film for a printing plate.

Overprinting: Printing one color over another to produce a new color.

Prepress Proofs: Made from film separations before the printing plate is made. Used to check accuracy of registration and colors.

Progressive Proofs: Proofs pulled in the order that the colors are added for printing. Colors are shown singly and in combination. Printer and production manager check color accuracy and ink density.

Registration: Perfect alignment of colors. Colors falling outside their intended borders are caused by misregistration.

Relief Printing: Raised surface printing. Ink is applied to a raised surface, meets paper under pressure, and then prints. Artists use relief methods when making woodcuts, wood engravings, linoleum cuts, and cardboard cuts. Letter-press printing is the commercial form of relief printing. It was at one time the most common way to print books and is still used for small editions.

Screen Tints: Dot patterns necessary in order to reproduce shades of black or colors. Original art is photographed through a finely ruled glass screen which breaks the image into the dots. Formerly called the Benday process.

Sewing: A book may be sewn together or bound by the following methods:
Side sewing: Thread passes through entire book in the gutter. Used on library editions for its durability.
Smyth sewing: Thread passes through the gutter of each signature or group of pages. As a result, the book opens more flat. Used on bookstore editions.
Perfect binding: Adhesives are used to bind pages together; used on paperbacks; least durable

Signature: Group of pages that are printed on the same press sheet, folded, cut, and sewn together to form a book. A standard picture book has two sixteen-page signatures. Signatures are in multiples of eight.

Specs: Instructions for the manufacturing of a book, including type of paper, printing inks, colors, weight of binding board, and type of binding.

Stripping: Positioning of films and art and text on supportive orange vinyl sheets in order to make the flats for the printing plates.

Trim Size: Final size of pages after press sheet has been folded and cut into signatures. Must be taken into consideration when choosing paper size for press sheet in order to avoid waste.

Resources

CHAPTER 1

Books

Each of the books selected presents a philosophy of literature and art for children unique to its author or authors. Reading these books will give you an excellent point of departure for forming your own philosophy about illustrating for children.

Bator, Robert. *Signposts to Criticism of Children's Literature*. Chicago: American Library Association, 1983.

Colby, Jean Pointdexter. *Writing, Editing, and Illustrating Children's Books*. New York: Hastings House, 1969.

Egoff, Shelia, G. Stubbs, and L. F. Ashley, eds. *Only Connect*. Toronto: Oxford University Press, 1980.

Haviland, Virginia. *Children's Literature Views and Reviews*. Chicago: Scott Foresman and Co., 1972.

Hearne, Betsy, and Marilyn Kaye, eds. *Celebrating Children's Books*. New York: Lothrop, Lee, and Shepard, 1981.

Hoffman, Miriam, and Eva Samuels. *Authors and Illustrators of Children's Books*. New York: R. R. Bowker Company, 1972.

Karl, Jean. *From Childhood to Childhood*. New York: John Day Company, 1970.

Kingman, Lee, ed. *The Illustrator's Notebook*. Boston: Horn Book, 1978.

Lanes, Selma. *Down the Rabbit Hole*. New York: Atheneum, 1971.

Schwarcz, Joseph. *The Ways of the Illustrator: Visual Communication in Children's Literature*. Chicago: American Library Association, 1983.

Illustration Awards

American Institute of Graphic Arts presents Best Book Awards for excellence of text and art, sponsors exhibits, publishes catalogs.

Boston Globe Horn Book awards are awarded annually to outstanding books in the categories of fiction and poetry, nonfiction, and illustration.

The Caldecott Medal is awarded annually by the Association for Library Service to Children to the most distinguished picture book published in the United States during the previous year.

The New York Times awards Choice of the Illustrated Children's Books of the Year for excellence in illustration.

Periodicals That Review Children's Books

Booklist. American Library Association. Reviews 1,000–4,000 recommended books annually and publishes an annual list of notable books.

The Bulletin. University of Chicago, Center for Children's Books. Reviews 400 books annually.

Horn Book. Horn Book, Inc. Reviews 400 books annually and contains excellent articles by authors and illustrators on various aspects of children's books. Publishes annual Fanfare list.

School Library Journal. R. R. Bowker Company. Reviews over 2,000 books annually and awards Best Books Award for originality and reader appeal.

CHAPTER 2

General Books on Learning to Draw

Goldstein, Nathan. *The Art of Responsive Drawing*, 3rd edition. Englewood Cliffs, N.J.: Prentice-Hall, Inc., 1984.

Hale, Robert Beverly. *Drawing Lessons from the Great Masters*. New York: Watson Guptill, 1964.

Kaupelis, Robert. *Learning to Draw*. New York: Watson Guptill, 1966.

Nelson, Roy P. *Humorous Illustration and Cartooning: A Guide for Editors, Advertisers, and Artists*. Englewood Cliffs, N.J.: Prentice-Hall, Inc., 1984.

Nicolaides, Kimon. *The Natural Way to Draw*. Boston: Houghton Mifflin, 1941.

Simmons, Seymour, and Marc Winer. *Drawing: The Creative Process*. Englewood Cliffs, N.J.: Prentice-Hall, Inc., 1977.

Watson, Ernest, and Aldren Watson. *The Watson Drawing Book*. New York: Bell Publishing, 1962.

Anatomy and Figure Drawing

Goldstein, Nathan. *Figure Drawing*. Englewood Cliffs, N.J.: Prentice-Hall, Inc., 1975.

Hale, William Beverly. *Anatomy Lessons from the Great Masters*. New York: Watson Guptill, 1977.

Hogarth, Burne. *Dynamic Anatomy*. New York: Watson Guptill, 1958.

Muybridge, Edward. *The Human Figure in Motion*. New York: Dover Publications, 1957.

Shider, Fritz. *An Atlas of Anatomy for Artists*. New York: Dover Publications, 1947.

Animals and Nature

Leslie, Claire Walker. *Nature Drawing: A Tool For Learning*. Englewood Cliffs, N.J.: Prentice-Hall, Inc., 1980.

Muybridge, Guy. *Animals in Motion*. Dover Publications, 1955.

Sweney, Frederic. *The Art of Painting Animals*. Englewood Cliffs, N.J.: Prentice-Hall, Inc., 1983.

Wilerding, Walter J. *Animal Drawing and Painting*. New York: Dover Publications, 1966.

Wilson, Maurice. *Drawing Animals*. New York: Watson Guptill, 1964.

Children and People

Hogarth, Paul. *Drawing People*. New York: Watson Guptill, 1971.

Marshall, Samuel. *How to Paint and Draw People*. New York: Cresent Books, 1981.

McArdle, Lois. *Portrait Drawing*. Englewood Cliffs, N.J.: Prentice-Hall, Inc., 1984.

Composition and Design

Landa, Robin. *An Introduction to Design*. Englewood Cliffs, N.J.: Prentice-Hall, Inc., 1983.

Lauer, David A. *Design Basics*. New York: Holt Rinehart and Winston, 1979.

Resnick, Elizabeth. *Graphic Design*. Englewood Cliffs, N.J.: Prentice-Hall, Inc., 1984.

Perspective and Volume

Hogarth, Burne. *Dynamic Light and Shade*. New York: Watson Guptill, 1981.

James, Jane H. *Perspective Drawing: A Directed Study*. Englewood Cliffs, N.J.: Prentice-Hall, Inc., 1981.

Watson, Ernest. *How to Use Creative Perspective*. New York: Van Nostrand Reinhold, 1955.

Environments

Gurney, James, and Thomas Kincade. *The Artist's Guide to Sketching: A Handbook for Drawing on the Spot*. New York: Watson Guptill, 1982.

Leslie, Claire Walker. *The Art of Field Sketching*. Englewood Cliffs, N.J.: Prentice-Hall, Inc., 1984.

Pitz, Henry. *Drawing Outdoors*. New York: Watson Guptill, 1977.

CHAPTER 3

Books

Ciancolo, Patricia. *Literature for Children: Illustrations in Children's Books*. Dubuque, Iowa: W. C. Brown, 1970.

Kingman, Lee, ed. *The Illustrator's Notebook*. Boston: Horn Book, 1978.

Klemin, Diana. *The Art of Art of Children's Books*. New York: Clarkson Potter, 1966.

Klemin, Diana. *The Illustrated Book: Its Art and Craft*. New York: Clarkson Potter, 1970.

Pitz, Henry. *Illustrating Children's Books*. New York: Watson Guptill, 1963.

Schwarcz, Joseph. *The Ways of the Illustrator*. Chicago: The American Library Association, 1982.

Books on Specific Techniques

Borgeson, Bet. *The Colored Pencil*. New York: Watson Guptill, 1983.

Borgman, Harry. *Drawing in Ink—Drawing for Reproduction*. New York: Watson Guptill, 1977.

Guptill, Arthur. *Drawing in Pen and Ink*. New York: Van Nostrand Reinhold, 1961.

Hogarth, Paul. *Creative Pencil Drawing*. New York: Watson Guptill, 1964.

Hogarth, Paul. *Creative Ink Drawing*. New York: Watson Guptill, 1968.

Simister. W. *How to Use Scratchboard*. New York: Drake Publishers, Inc., 1972.

Films and Filmstrips

Weston Woods Signature Collection of Motion Pictures and Filmstrips presents a selection of noted illustrators working in their studios and discussing their work. These are available through public and school libraries. Artists include: Edward Ardizonne; Randolph Caldecott; James Daugherty; Gail E. Haley; Ezra Jack Keats; Steven Kellogg; Robert McCloskey; Gerald McDermott; Maurice Sendak; and Tomi Ungerer.

CHAPTER 5

Books and Periodicals

Ciancola, Patricia, ed. *Picture Books for Children*. Chicago: American Library Association and National Council of Teachers of English, 1973. Includes excellent bibliography.

McCann, Donna Rae, and Olga Richard. *The Child's First Books*. New York: H. W. Wilson and Co., 1973.

Hearne, Betsy, and Marilyn Kaye. *Celebrating Children's Books* New York: Lothrop, Lee, and Shepard, 1981. Chapter by Arnold Lobel.

Roberts, Ellen. *The Children's Picture Book: How to Write It, How To Sell It*. Cincinnati: Writer's Digest, 1982. Includes bibliography and good information for artists as well as writers.

Shulevitz, Uri. "Within the Margins of a Picturebook," *Horn Book,* June 1971. pp. 134–35.

Shulevitz, Uri. "What is a Picturebook?" *Wilson Library Bulletin,* October 1980, pp. 99–101.

Films and Filmstrips

The Lively Art of the Picture Book. Weston Woods Studios.

The Signature Collection. Weston Woods Studios.

CHAPTER 6

Books

Arnold, Edmund. *Ink on Paper*. Englewood Cliffs, N.J.: Prentice-Hall, Inc., 1972.

Chappell, Warren. *A Short History of the Printed Word*. New York: Knopf, 1970.

Frank, Susan, and Mindy Levine. *In Print: A Concise Guide to Graphic Printing for Small Business and Non-Profit Organizations*. Englewood Cliffs, N.J.: Prentice-Hall, Inc., 1984.

Greenfield, Howard. *Books From Writer to Reader*. New York: Crown Publishers, Inc., 1976.

International Paper Company. *Pocket Pal,*

latest edition. Periodic printings provide updated information.

Lee, Marshall. *Bookmaking, the Illustrated Guide to Design, Production, and Editing*. New York: R. R. Bowker, 1979.

Periodicals

American Printer. Chicago, Ill.: MacClean Hunter Publishing Group.

Graphic Arts Monthly. New York, N.Y.

CHAPTER 7

Books

Cardamonne, Tom. *Mechanical Color Separation Skills for the Commercial Artist*. New York: Van Nostrand Reinhold, 1980.

Craig, James. *Production for the Graphic Designer*. New York: Watson Guptill, 1974.

Gates, David. *Graphic Design Studio Procedures*. New York: Lloyd Simone, 1982.

Gray, Bill. *Studio Tips for the Graphic Designer*. New York: Van Nostrand Reinhold, 1976.

Thoma Marta. *Graphic Illustration*. Englewood Cliffs, N.J.: Prentice-Hall, Inc., 1982.

Simon, Hilda. *Color in Reproduction*. New York: The Viking Press, 1980.

Materials and Tools

Goodchild, Jon, and Bill Henkin. *By Design*. New York: Quick Fox, 1980. Lists mail order companies, books, special art materials, studio equipment, periodicals.

Grumbacher, M. *Dial A Color Wheel*.

Lem, Dean. *Graphics Master 2,* latest edition. Los Angeles: Dean Lem Associates.

Letraset. *Pantone Color Reference Manuals*. Available at art supply stores.

Simon, Hilda. *Color in Reproduction.* New York: The Viking Press, 1980. See pages 82–86 for color charts.
PMS color charts, available through printers.

Mail Order Art Suppliers

Flax Art Supplies. Chicago, New York, Phoenix, San Francisco.
A. I. Friedman, 25 W. 45th Street, New York, N.Y. 10036.

CHAPTER 8

General Books

Balkin, Richard. *A Writer's Guide to Book Publishing.* New York: E. P. Dutton, 1977.
Dessauer, John. *Book Publishing: What It Is, What It Does.* New York: 1974.
Mayer, Debbie. *Literary Agents, A Writer's Guide.* New York: Poets and Writers, 1983.
Meyer, Caroline. *The Writer's Survival Manual.* New York: Crown Publishers, Inc., 1982.

Editing and Writing Children's Books

Aiken, Joan. *The Way to Write for Children.* New York: St. Martin's Press, 1982.
Colby, Jean Pointdexter. *Writing, Editing, and Illustrating Children's Books,* New York: Hastings House: 1970.
Karl Jean. *From Childhood to Childhood.* New York: John Day Co., 1970.
Roberts, Ellen. *The Children's Picturebook: How to Write It, How to Sell It.* Cincinnati: Writer's Digest, 1982.
Seuling, Barbara. *How to Write A Children's Book.* New York: Scribner's, 1984.
Wyndham, Lee. *Writing for Children and Teenagers.* Cincinnati: Writer's Digest, 1980.

Yolen, Jane. *Writing Books for Children.* Boston: The Writer, 1982.

Reference Books

Artist's Market. Cincinnati: Writer's Digest. Updated annually.
Literary Market Place. New York: R. R. Bowker Company. Updated annually.
International Directory of Little Magazines and Small Presses. Paradise: Dust Books. Updated annually.
Publisher's Trade List Annual. New York: R. R. Bowker. Annual compilation of publisher's catalogs.
Writer's Market. Cincinnati: Writer's Digest. Annual edition includes publishers' names and addresses.

Associations

Author's Guild, 23 W. 43rd St. New York, N.Y. 10036. Provides services to authors.
Children's Book Council, 67 Irving Place, New York, N.Y. 10003. Provides list of materials about children's books which they publish (enclose SASE). Sponsors Children's Book Week and Every Child convention.
Poets and Writers, 201 W. 54th St. New York, N.Y. 10019. Publishes pamphlets and newsletters helpful to writers.
Society of Children's Book Writers, P.O. Box 296, Mar Vista Station, Calif. 90066. Monthly newsletters include annual market survey of publisher's needs.

CHAPTER 9

Books

Appelbaum, Stanley. *Bizzaries and Fantasies of Grandville.* New York: Dover Publications, 1974.

Bader, Barbara. *American Picturebooks from Noah's Ark to the Beast Within.* Macmillan Publishing Company, 1976.

Billington, Elizabeth, ed. *The Randolph Caldecott Treasury.* New York: Frederick Warne and Co., Inc., 1978.

Bland, David. *A History of Book Illustration.* Cleveland: World Publishing Company, 1938.

Brooke, Henry. *Leslie Brooke and Johnny Crow.* New York: Frederick Warne and Co., Inc., 1982.

Brown, John Buchanan. *The Book Illustrations of George Cruikshank.* Rutland: Charles E. Tuttle Company, 1980.

Feaver, William. *When We Were Very Young: Two Centuries of Children's Book Illustration.* New York: Holt Rinehart and Winston, 1977.

Lane, Margaret. *The Magic Years of Beatrix Potter.* New York: Frederick Warne and Co., Inc., 1978.

Lee, Kingman, Grace Allen Hogarth and Harriet Quimby. *Illustrators of Children's Books: 1967–1976* Boston: Horn Book, Inc. Also see editions of 1744–1945, 1946–1956, and 1957–1966.

Jones, Helen. *Robert Lawson, Illustrator.* Boston: Little Brown and Company, 1972.

McKenden, John, ed. *Five Centuries of Illustrated Fables.* New York: Metropolitan Museum of Art, 1964.

Pierpont Morgan Library. *Early Children's Books and Their Illustration.* Boston: David Godine, 1975.

Pitz, Henry. *A Treasury of American Book Illustration.* New York: Watson Guptill and American Studio Books, 1947.

Simon, Howard. *Five Hundred Years of Art and Illustration.* Cleveland: The World Publishing Company, 1942.

Smith, Dora. *Fifty Years of Children's Books: 1910–1960.* Champaign, Ill.: National Council of Teachers of English, 1963.

Colleges that Offer Courses

If you would like to pursue further study of children's book illustration, several colleges offer courses. Write for further information.

Appalachia State University, Boone, NC. 28608. Special arrangement with Gail E. Haley.

California College of Arts and Crafts, Oakland CA, 94606. Semester Course.

Hartwick College, Oneonta, NY. Summer program: workshop in the illustration and writing of children's books.

The New School for Social Research, 66 West 12th Street, New York, NY 10011. Semester course.

Parsons School of Design, 66 Fifth Avenue, New York, NY 10011. Semester course.

School for the Visual Arts, 209 East 23rd Street, New York, NY 10010. Semester course.

Split Rock Arts Program, 77 Pleasant Street S.E., Minneapolis, MN 55455. Summer workshops.

Syracuse University, Syracuse, NY 13201. Semester course.

University of Santa Cruz, Santa Cruz, CA 95064. Summer workshop.

Index

Credits